ukulele
all-time
favorites

Amsco Publications
part of *The Music Sales Group*
London/New York/Paris/Sydney/Copenhagen/Berlin/Madrid/Tokyo

Exclusive Distributors:
Music Sales Corporation
257 Park Avenue South, New York, NY 10010 USA
Music Sales Limited,
14-15 Berners Street, London W1T 3LJ, UK.
Music Sales Pty Limited,
20 Resolution Drive, Caringbah, NSW 2229, Australia.

Order No. AM994004
ISBN 978-0-8256-3630-1

Edited by David Harrison.
Cover designed by Fresh Lemon.
Photographs courtesy of Matthew Ward.

Printed in the United States of America.

Your Guarantee of Quality
As publishers, we strive to produce every book to the highest
commercial standards.

The music has been freshly engraved and the book has been carefully designed
to minimize awkward page turns and to make playing from it a real pleasure.

Particular care has been given to specifying acid-free, neutral-sized
paper made from pulps which have not been elemental chlorine bleached.

This pulp is from farmed sustainable forests and was produced with
special regard for the environment.

Throughout, the printing and binding have been planned to ensure
a sturdy, attractive publication which should give years of enjoyment.

If your copy fails to meet our high standards, please inform us
and we will gladly replace it.

www.musicsales.com

amazing grace

Words by John Newton
Music traditional American

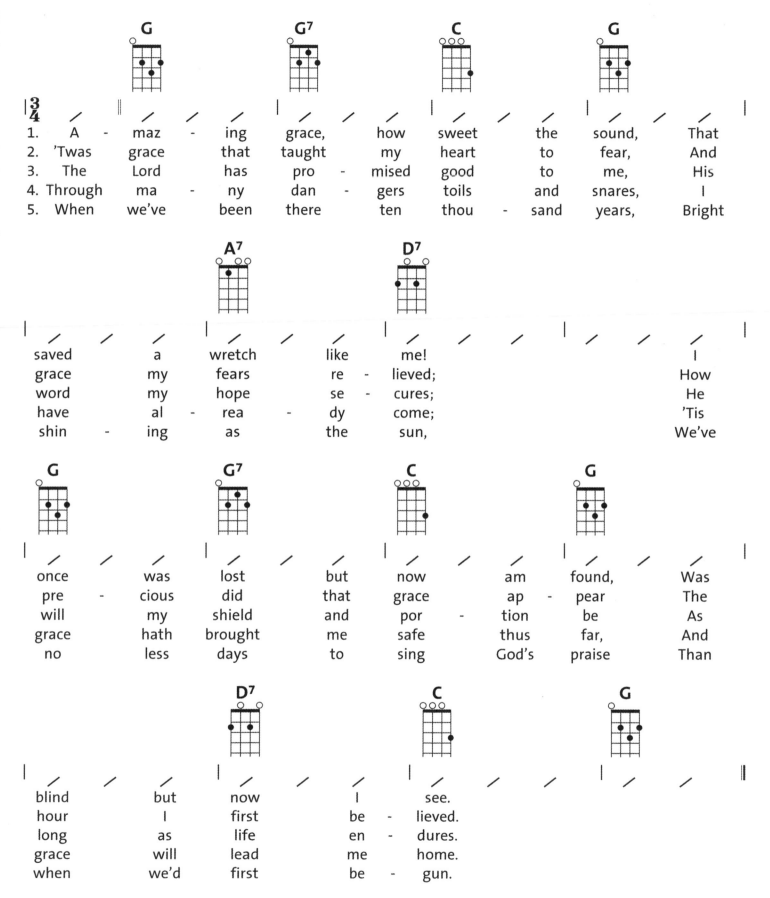

the big rock candy mountain

American hobo song

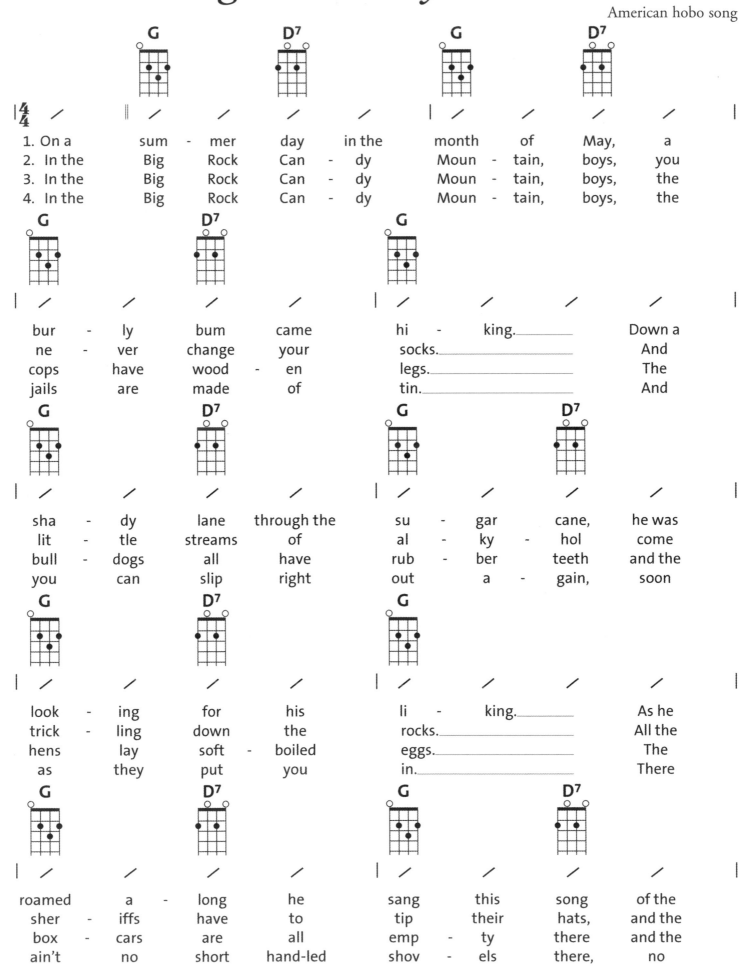

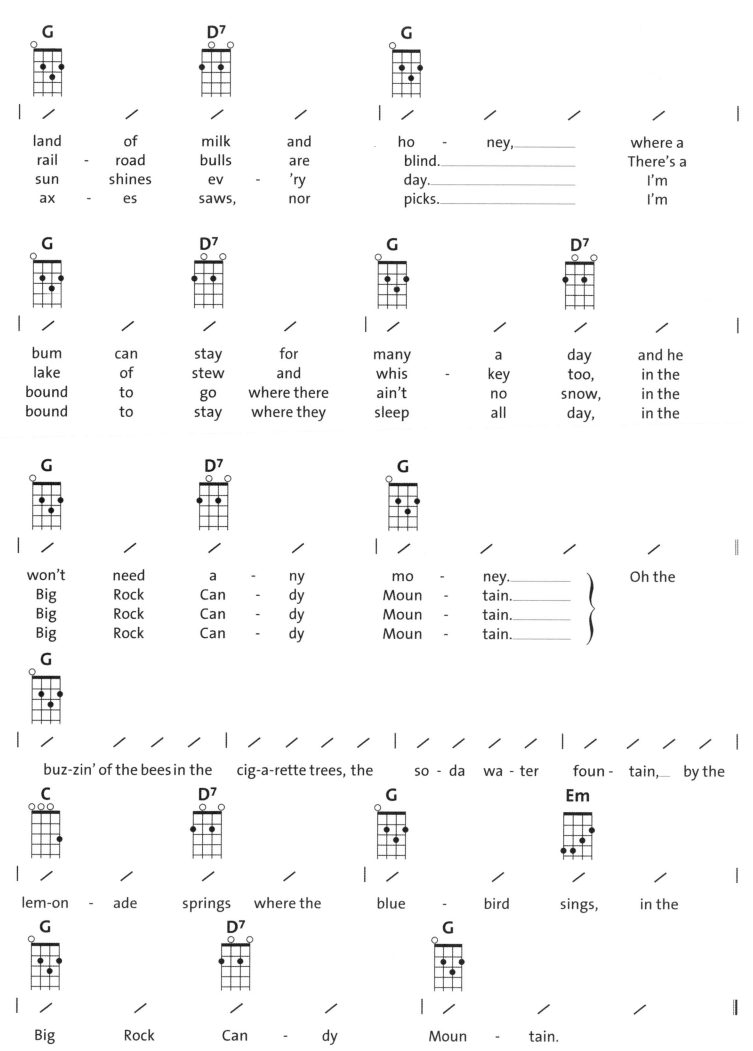

camptown races

Words and Music by Stephen C. Foster

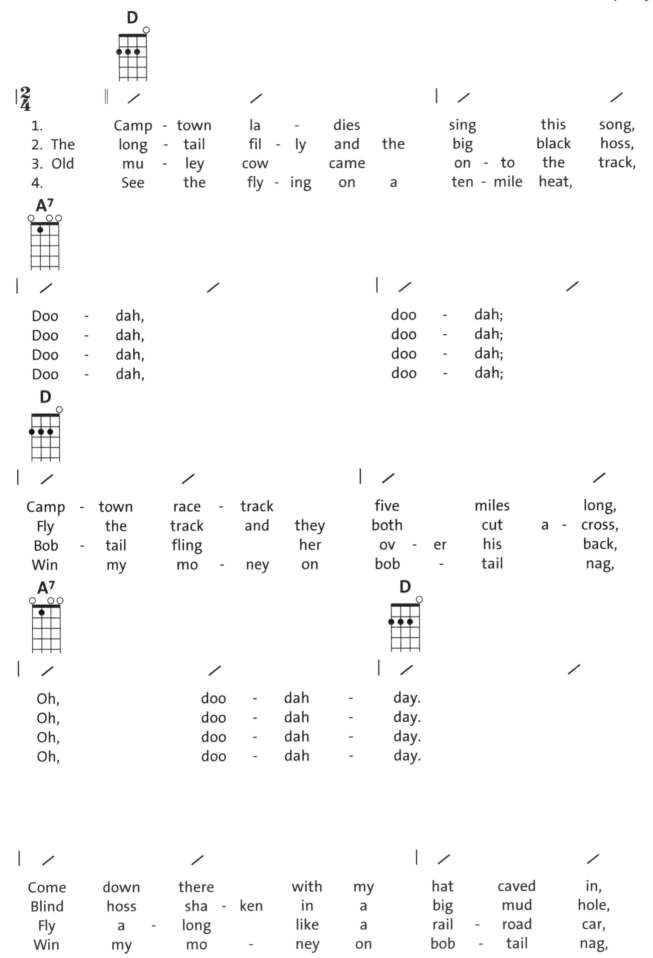

A⁷

Doo - dah,   doo - dah;
Doo - dah,   doo - dah;
Doo - dah,   doo - dah;
Doo - dah,   doo - dah;

D

Go   back   home   with my   pock - et   full   of   tin,
Can't   touch   bot - tom with a   ten - foot   pole,
Run - ning   a   race   with   a   shoot - ing   star,
Keep   my   mo - ney   in   an   old   tow   bag,

A⁷   **D**

Oh,   doo - dah - day.
Oh,   doo - dah - day.
Oh,   doo - dah - day.
Oh,   doo - dah - day.

D   **G**   **D**

Goin'   to run all   night,   Goin'   to run all   day,

D   **A⁷**   **D**

Bet my mo-ney on the   bob - tail nag;   Some-bo-dy bet on the   bay.

danny boy

Words by Frederic E. Weatherly
Music traditional Irish

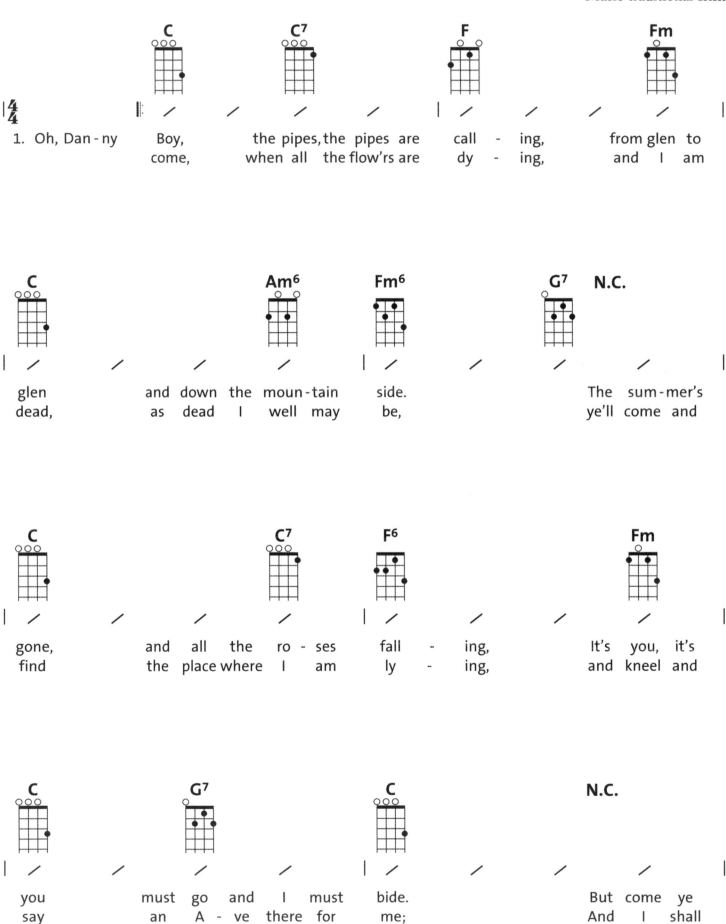

1. Oh, Dan - ny   Boy,   the pipes, the pipes are   call - ing,   from glen to
                  come,   when all   the flow'rs are   dy - ing,   and I am

glen   and down the moun - tain side.   The sum - mer's
dead,   as dead I well may   be,   ye'll come and

gone,   and all the ro - ses   fall - ing,   It's you, it's
find   the place where I am   ly - ing,   and kneel and

you   must go and I must   bide.   But come ye
say   an A - ve there for   me;   And I shall

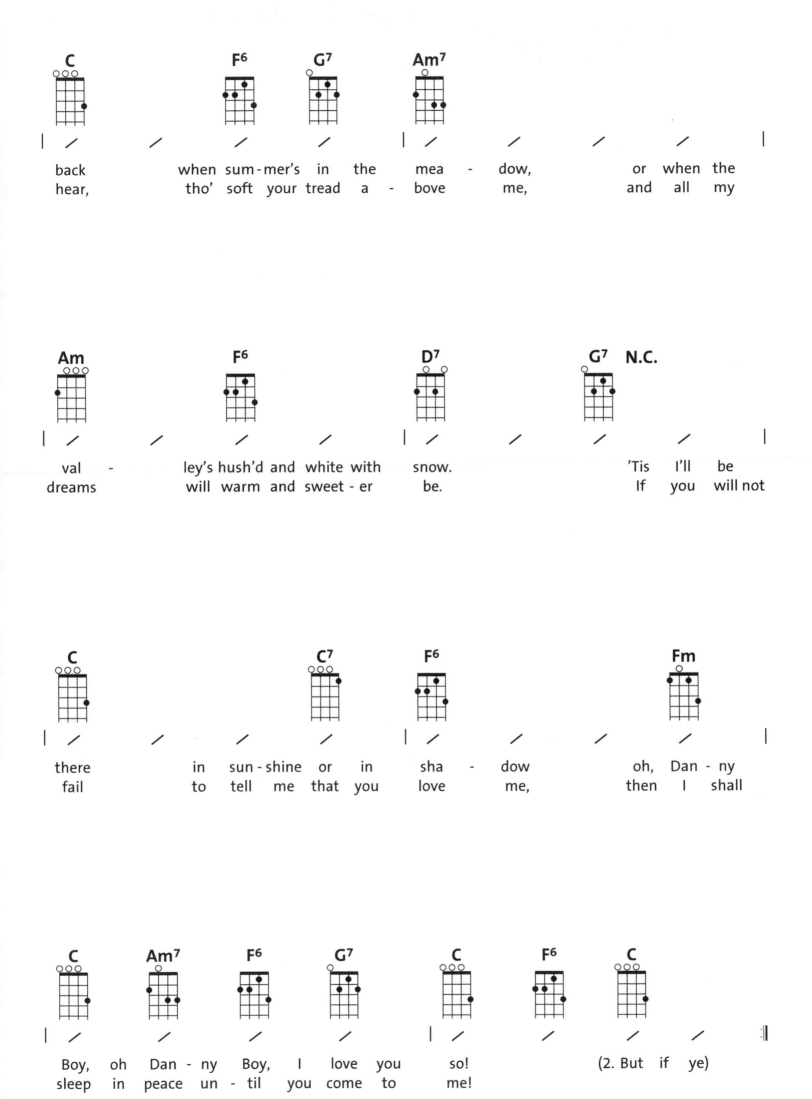

C   F⁶   G⁷   Am⁷

| / | / | / | / | / | / | / | / |

back   when sum-mer's in the   mea - dow,   or when the
hear,   tho' soft your tread a - bove me,   and all my

Am   F⁶   D⁷   G⁷   N.C.

| / | / | / | / | / | / | / | / |

val -   ley's hush'd and white with   snow.   'Tis   I'll   be
dreams   will warm and sweet - er   be.   If   you   will not

C   C⁷   F⁶   Fm

| / | / | / | / | / | / | / | / |

there   in sun - shine or in   sha - dow   oh, Dan - ny
fail   to tell me that you   love me,   then I shall

C   Am⁷   F⁶   G⁷   C   F⁶   C

| / | / | / | / | / | / | / | / |

Boy,   oh   Dan - ny   Boy,   I   love   you   so!   (2. But if ye)
sleep   in   peace   un - til   you   come   to   me!

9

dixie

Words and Music by Daniel Decatur Emmett

C

1. I	wish I	was in the	land of	cot - ton
2. Old	Mis - sus mar - ry	Will the	Wea - ver,	
3. His	face was sharp as a	butch - er's	clea - ver,	
4. Now	here's a health to the	next old	Mis - sus and	

F

old	times there are	not for - got - ten.	Look a -
Wil - liam	was a	gay de - cei - ver.	Look a -
but	that did not	seem to grieve her.	Look a -
all	the girls that	want to kiss us.	Look a -

C   **G**   **C**

- way,	Look a - way, look a - way,	Dix - ie Land!	In
- way,	Look a - way, look a - way,	Dix - ie Land!	But
- way,	Look a - way, look a - way,	Dix - ie Land!	Old
- way,	Look a - way, look a - way,	Dix - ie Land!	But

Dix - ie Land	where	I was born in
when he put	his	arm a - round her, he
Mis - sus act - ed the	fool -	ish part and
if you want to drive a -	way the	sor - row,

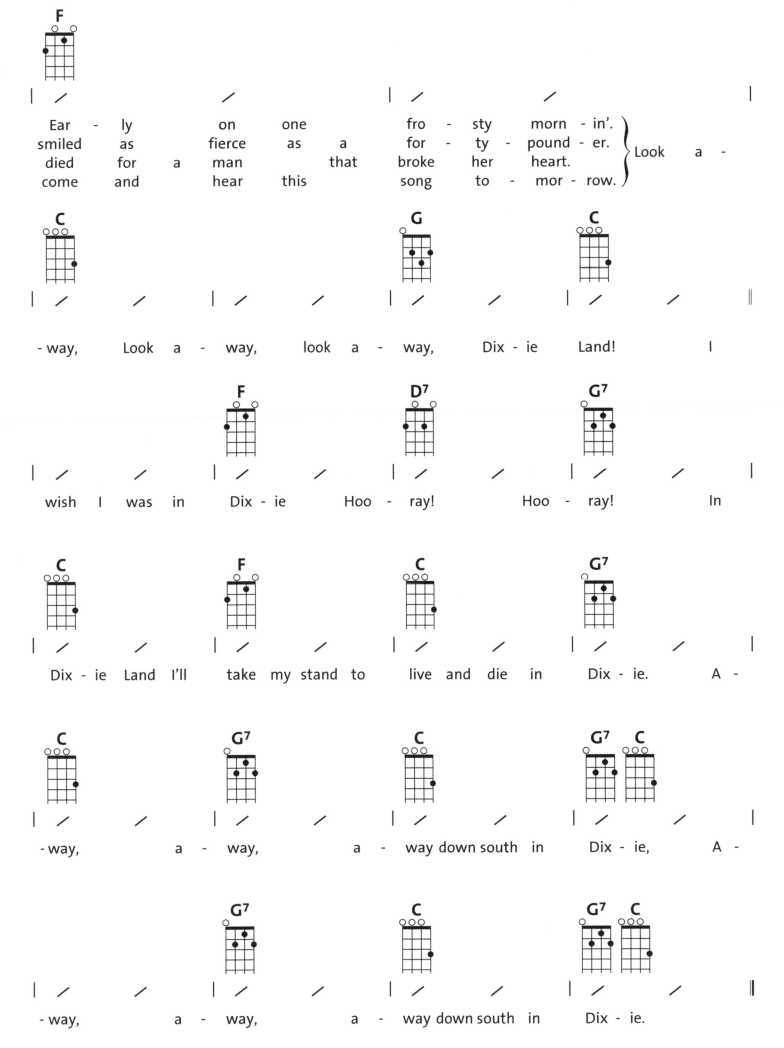

down by the riverside

African-American spiritual

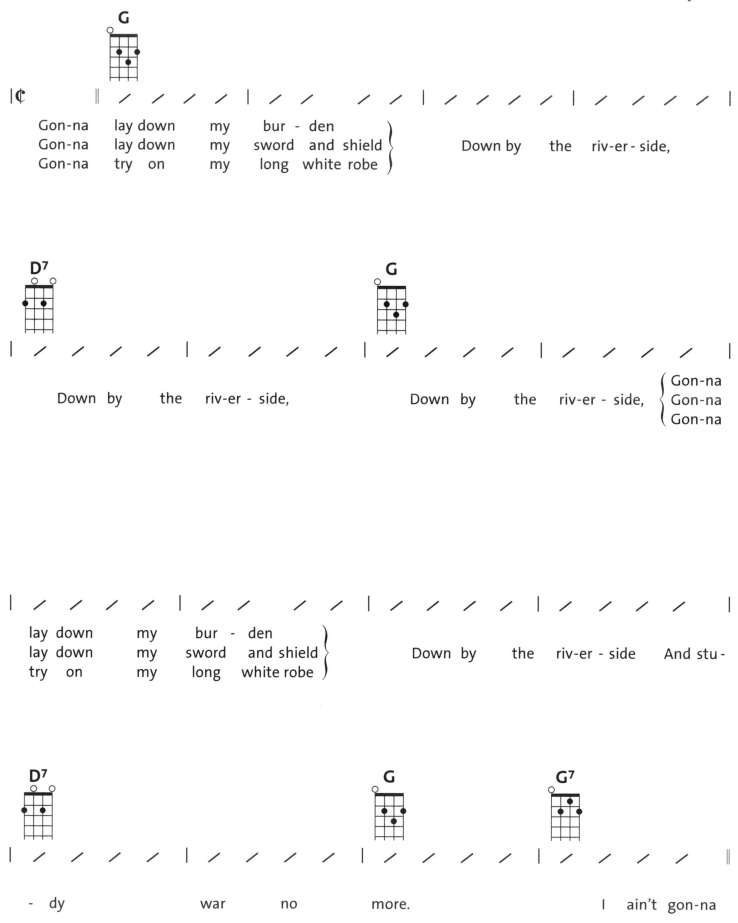

Gon-na   lay down   my   bur - den
Gon-na   lay down   my   sword   and shield   Down by   the   riv-er - side,
Gon-na   try on   my   long   white robe

Down by   the   riv-er - side,   Down by   the   riv-er - side,   Gon-na
Gon-na
Gon-na

lay down   my   bur - den
lay down   my   sword   and shield   Down by   the   riv-er - side   And stu-
try on   my   long   white robe

- dy   war   no   more.   I   ain't gon-na

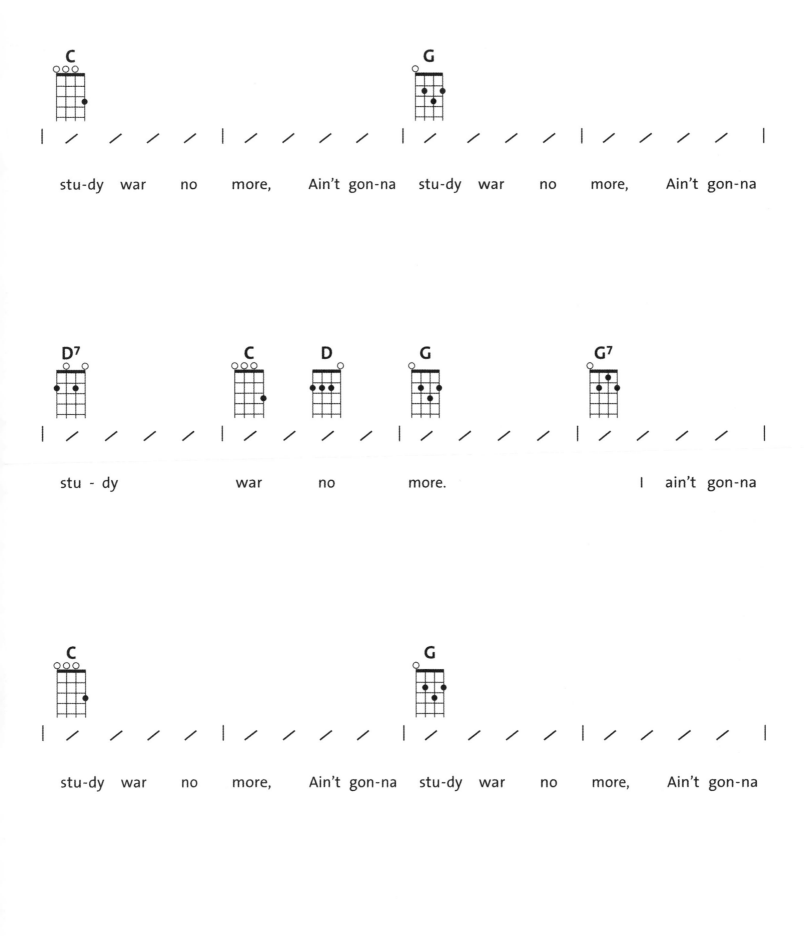

| C | | | | G | | | |

stu-dy war no more, Ain't gon-na stu-dy war no more, Ain't gon-na

| D⁷ | | C | D | G | | G⁷ |

stu - dy war no more. I ain't gon-na

| C | | | G | | |

stu-dy war no more, Ain't gon-na stu-dy war no more, Ain't gon-na

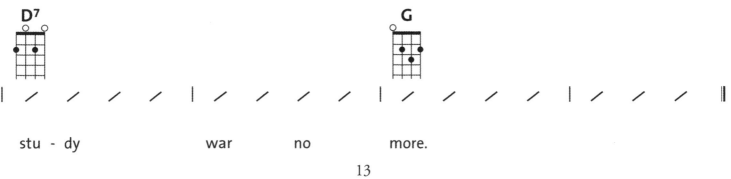

| D⁷ | | G | |

stu - dy war no more.

drunken sailor

American sea shanty

Dm

| 2/4 / | / | / | / | |

1. What shall we do with the drunk - en sail - or,
2. Put him in the long - boat till he's so - ber,
3. Put him in the scup - pers with the hose - pipe on him,
4. Tie him up in a run - ning bow - line,

C

| / | / | / | / | |

What shall we do with the drunk - en sail - or,
Put him in the long - boat till he's so - ber,
Put him in the scup - pers with the hose - pipe on him,
Tie him up in a run - ning bow - line,

Dm

| / | / | / | / | |

What shall we do with the drunk - en sail - or,
Put him in the long - boat till he's so - ber,
Put him in the scup -pers with the hose - pipe on him,
Tie him up in a run - ning bow - line,

C   **Dm**

| / | / | / | ‖

Ear - ly in the mor - ning.

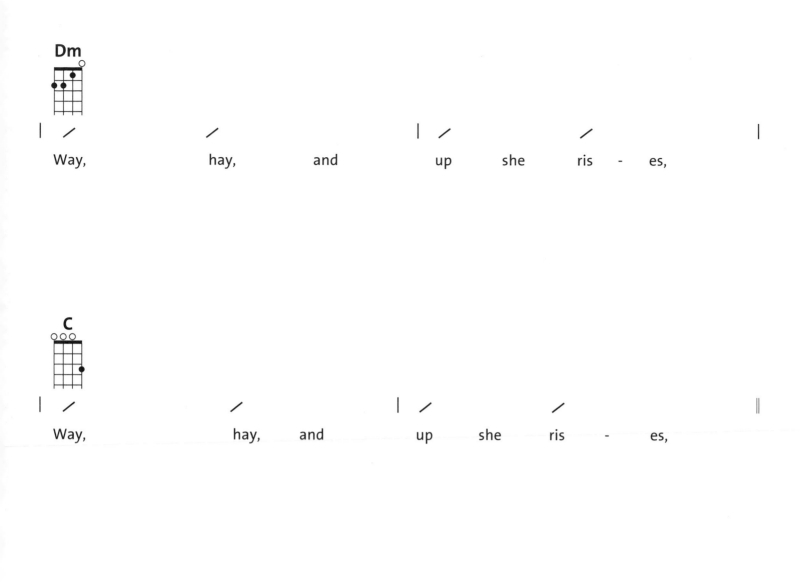

Dm

| /   / | /   / |

Way,   hay,   and   up   she   ris   -   es,

C

| /   / | /   /   ‖

Way,   hay,   and   up   she   ris   -   es,

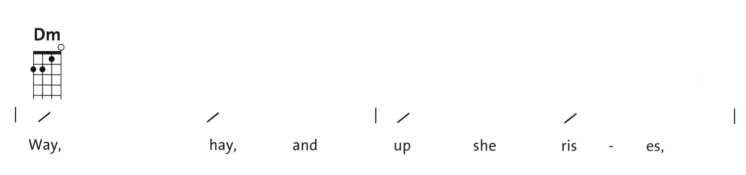

Dm

| /   / | /   / |

Way,   hay,   and   up   she   ris   -   es,

C   Dm

| /   / | /   /   ‖

Ear   -   ly   in   the   mor   -   ning.

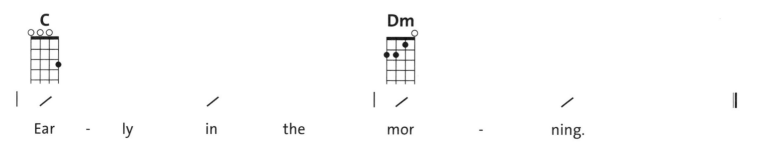

careless love

American folksong

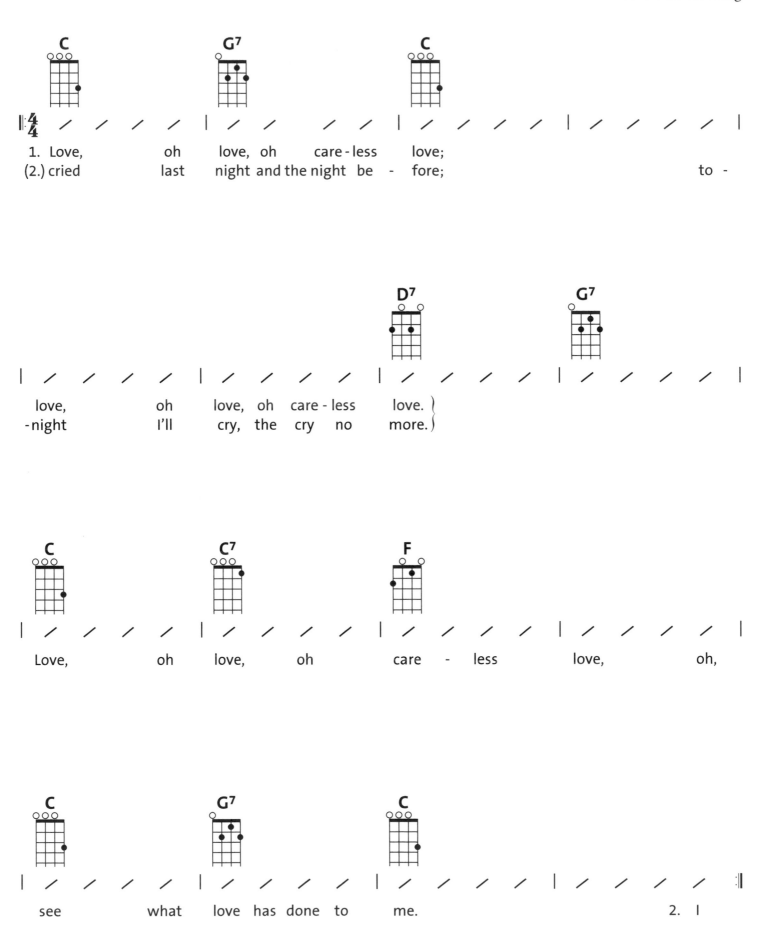

1. Love, oh love, oh care-less love;
(2.) cried last night and the night be - fore; to -

love, oh love, oh care-less love.⎞
-night I'll cry, the cry no more.⎠

Love, oh love, oh care - less love, oh,

see what love has done to me. 2. I

early one morning

English folksong

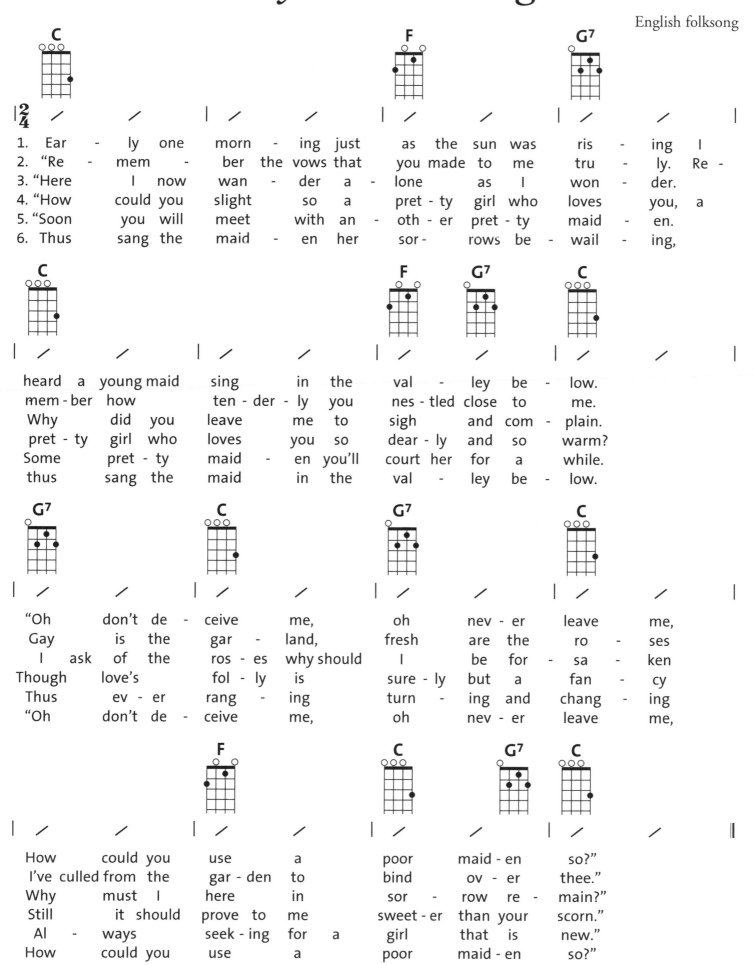

1. Ear - ly one morn - ing just as the sun was ris - ing
2. "Re - mem - ber the vows that you made to me tru - ly. Re -
3. "Here I now wan - der a - lone as I won - der.
4. "How could you slight so a pret - ty girl who loves you, a
5. "Soon you will meet with an - oth - er pret - ty maid - en.
6. Thus sang the maid - en her sor - rows be - wail - ing,

heard a young maid sing in the val - ley be - low.
mem - ber how ten - der - ly you nes - tled close to me.
Why did you leave me to sigh and com - plain.
pret - ty girl who loves you so dear - ly and so warm?
Some pret - ty maid - en you'll court her for a while.
thus sang the maid in the val - ley be - low.

"Oh don't de - ceive me, oh nev - er leave me,
Gay is the gar - land, fresh are the ro - ses
I ask of the ros - es why should I be for - sa - ken
Though love's fol - ly is sure - ly but a fan - cy
Thus ev - er rang - ing turn - ing and chang - ing
"Oh don't de - ceive me, oh nev - er leave me,

How could you use a poor maid - en so?"
I've culled from the gar - den to bind ov - er thee."
Why must I here in sor - row re - main?"
Still it should prove to me sweet - er than your scorn."
Al - ways seek - ing for a girl that is new."
How could you use a poor maid - en so?"

for he's a jolly good fellow

English folksong

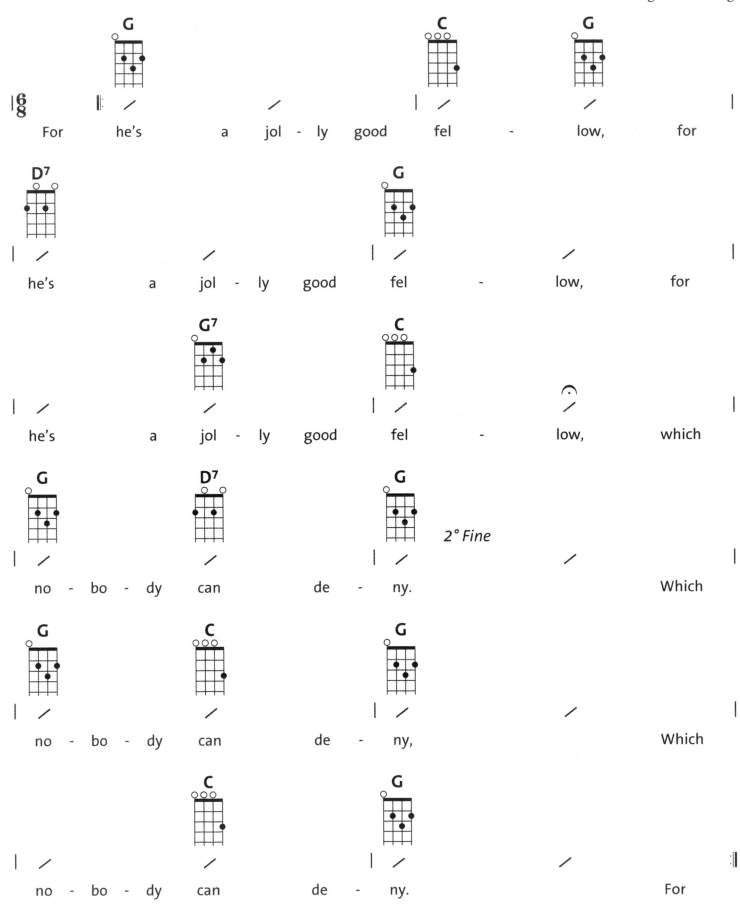

frankie and johnny

Anonymous blues ballad

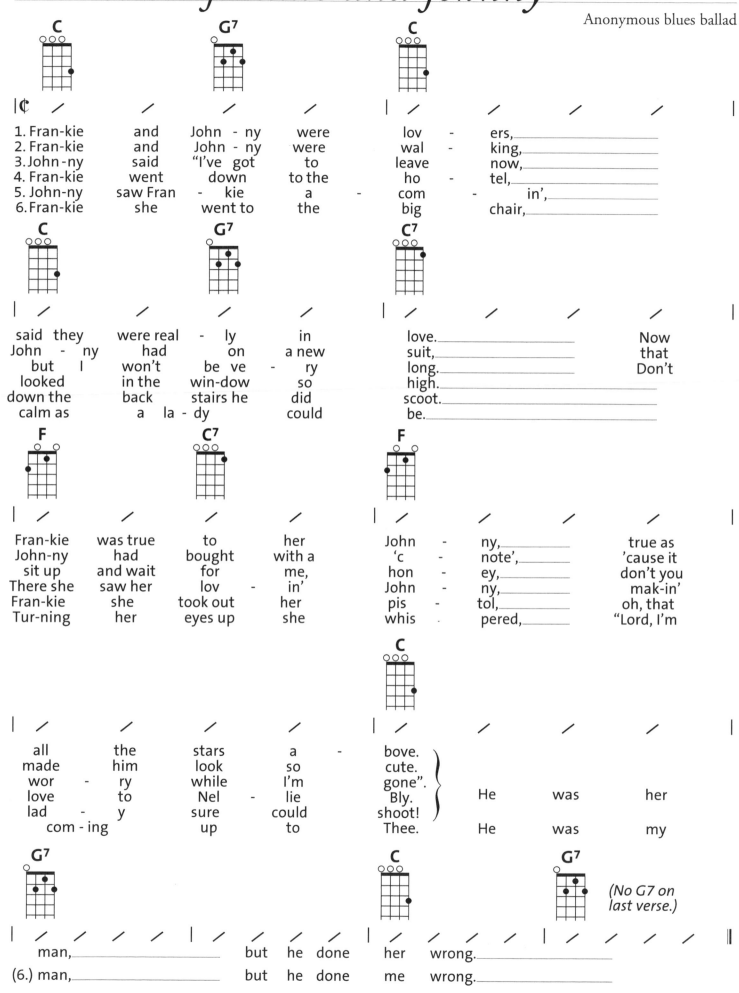

1. Fran-kie and John-ny were lov - ers, said they were real - ly in love. Now that Fran-kie was true to her John - ny, true as all the stars a - bove. He was her man, but he done her wrong.

2. Fran-kie and John-ny were wal - king, John - ny had on a new suit, that John-ny 'c - note', 'cause it made him look so cute.

3. John-ny said "I've got to leave now, but I won't be ve - ry long. There she sit up and wait for lov - in' hon - ey, don't you wor - ry while I'm sure I could love to Nel - lie up to.

4. Fran-kie went down to the ho - tel, looked in the win-dow so high. John-ny saw her took out her pis - tol, John - ny mak-in' lad - y, she took out her eyes up to shoot! Thee.

5. John-ny saw Fran - kie a - com - in', down the back stairs he did scoot. Fran-kie saw her she took out her pis - tol, whis - pered, oh, that lad - y, she could up to.

6. Fran-kie she went to the big chair, calm as a la - dy could be. Tur-ning her eyes up she whis - pered, "Lord, I'm com - ing Thee. He was my man,

(6.) man, but he done me wrong.

(No G7 on last verse.)

go down, moses

Traditional American spiritual

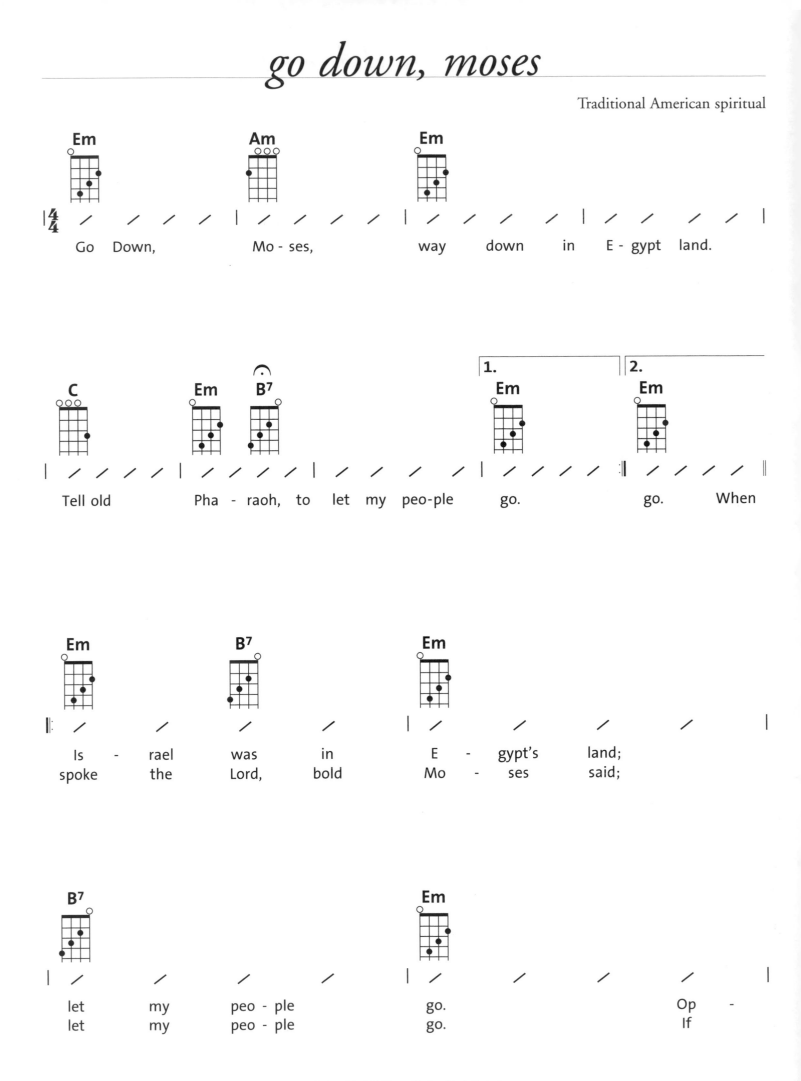

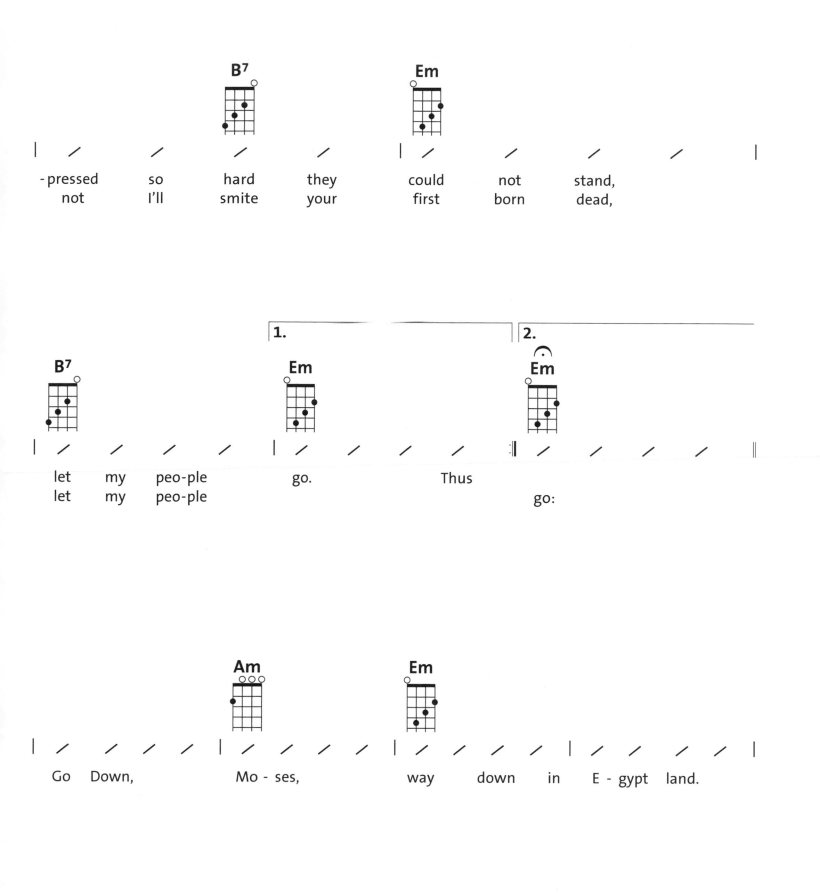

B7   **Em**

| /   /   /   / | /   /   /   / |

-pressed   so   hard   they   could   not   stand,
not   I'll   smite   your   first   born   dead,

B7   **1.**   **Em**   **2.**   **Em**

| /   /   /   / | /   /   /   / | /   /   /   / |

let   my   peo-ple   go.   Thus
let   my   peo-ple   go:

Am   **Em**

| /   /   /   / | /   /   /   / | /   /   /   / | /   /   /   / |

Go   Down,   Mo - ses,   way   down   in   E - gypt   land.

C   **Em**   **B7**   **Em**

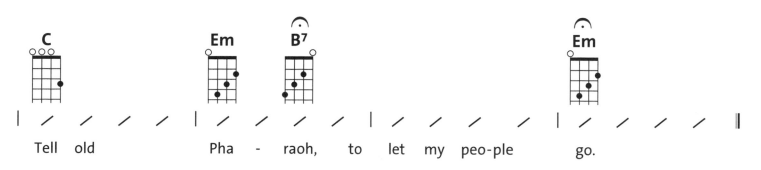

| /   /   /   / | /   /   /   / | /   /   /   / | /   /   /   / |

Tell   old   Pha - raoh,   to   let   my   peo-ple   go.

grandfather's clock

Words and Music by Henry Clay Work

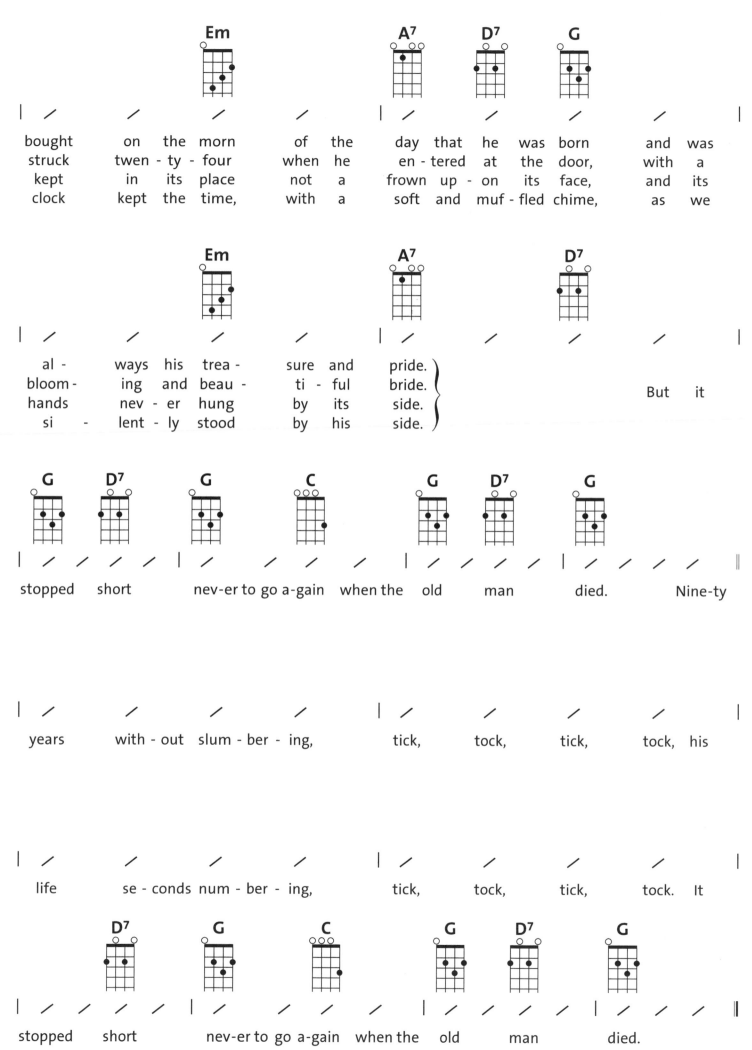

Em   A⁷   D⁷   G

bought   on   the   morn   of   the   day   that   he   was   born   and   was
struck   twen - ty - four   when   he   en - tered   at   the   door,   with   a
kept   in   its   place   not   a   frown   up - on   its   face,   and   its
clock   kept   the   time,   with   a   soft   and   muf - fled   chime,   as   we

Em   A⁷   D⁷

al -   ways   his   trea -   sure   and   pride.
bloom -   ing   and   beau -   ti - ful   bride.
hands   nev - er   hung   by   its   side.
si -   lent - ly   stood   by   his   side.   But   it

G   D⁷   G   C   G   D⁷   G

stopped   short   nev-er to go a-gain   when the   old   man   died.   Nine-ty

years   with - out   slum - ber - ing,   tick,   tock,   tick,   tock,   his

life   se - conds num - ber - ing,   tick,   tock,   tick,   tock.   It

D⁷   G   C   G   D⁷   G

stopped   short   nev-er to go a-gain   when the   old   man   died.

home on the range

Words by Dr. Brewster Higley
Music by Dan Kelly

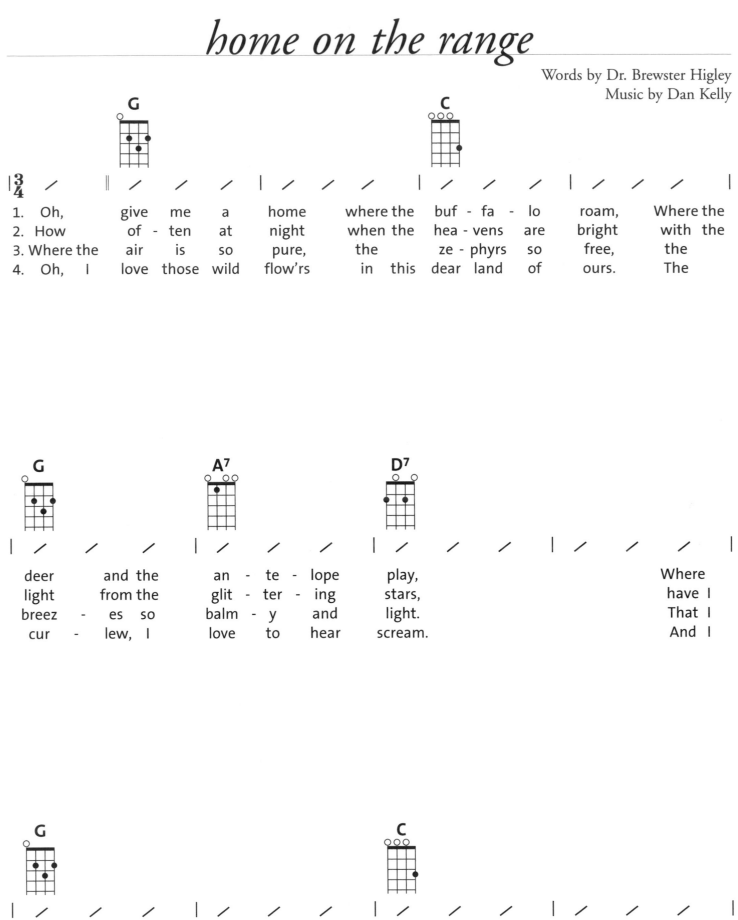

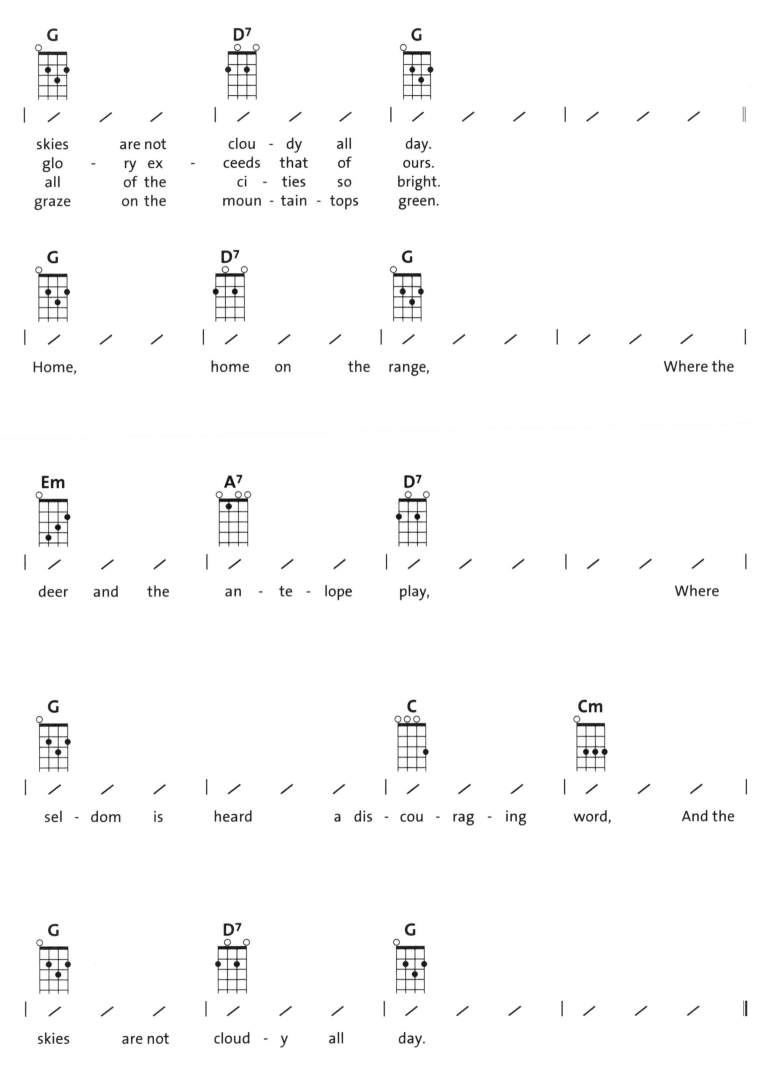

greensleeves

16th Century English

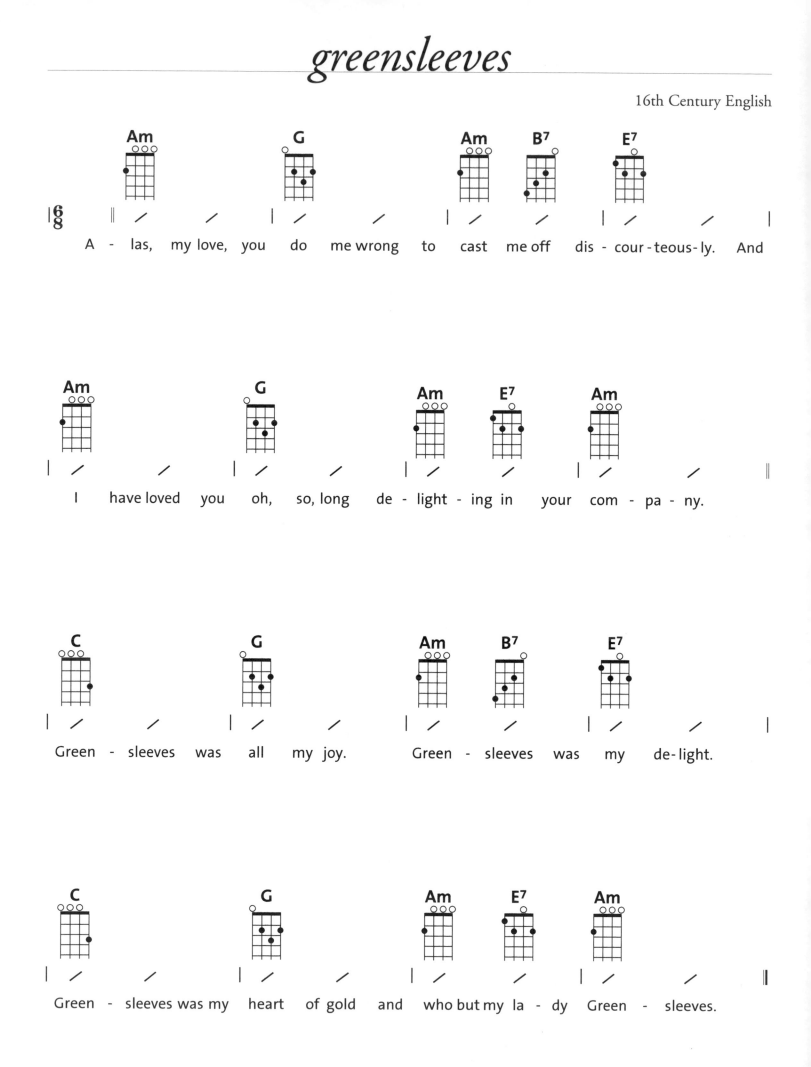

house of the rising sun

American folksong

Am

C

D

F

$\frac{3}{4}$ ╱ │ ╱ ╱ │ ╱ ╱ │ ╱ ╱ │ ╱ ╱ │

1. There is a house in New Or - leans, They
2. If I had lis - tened to what ma - ma had said, I'd 'a'
3. My mo - ther, she's a tai - lor, She
4. The on - ly thing a drunk - ard needs Is a
5. Go tell my ba - by, sis - ter, Ne - ver
6. One foot is on the plat - form, And the
7. I'm go - ing back to New Or - leans, My

Am

C

E⁷

│ ╱ ╱ ╱ │ ╱ ╱ ╱ │ ╱ ╱ ╱ │ ╱ ╱ ╱ │

call the Ris - ing Sun. It has
been at home to - day. My
sells those new blue jeans. The
suit - case and a trunk. To
do like I have done. I'm
oth - er is on the train.
race is al - most run.

Am

C

D

F

│ ╱ ╱ ╱ │ ╱ ╱ ╱ │ ╱ ╱ ╱ │ ╱ ╱ ╱ │

been the ru - in of ma-ny a poor girl, And
Be - ing so young and fool - ish, poor girl, Let a
sweet - heart, he's a drunk - ard Lord, Drink
on - ly time he's sa - tis - fied Is
shun that house in New Or - leans, They
go - ing back to New Or - leans To
Go - ing back to end my life Be -

Am

E⁷

Am

│ ╱ ╱ ╱ │ ╱ ╱ ╱ │ ╱ ╱ ╱ │ ╱ ╱ ╱ ‖

I, oh Lord, was one.
gam - bler lead me a - stray.
down in New Or - leans.
when he's on a drunk.
call the Ris - ing Sun.
wear the ball and chain.
-neath the Ris - ing Sun.

john brown's body

19th Century American

G

/	/	/	/	/	/	/	/

1. John   Brown's   bo - dy   lies   a - mould-'ring   in   the   grave,
2. The   stars   of   hea - ven   are   look - ing   kind - ly   down,
3. gone   to   be   a   sol - dier   in   the   ar - my   of   the   Lord,   He's
4. John   Brown   died   that   the   slave   might   be   free,
5. John   Brown's   knap - sack   is   strapped   to   his   back,
6. His   pet   lambs   will   meet   on   the   way,
7. They   will   hang   Jeff   Da - vis   on   a   sour   ap - ple   tree,

C   **G**

/	/	/	/	/	/	/	/

John   Brown's   bo - dy   lies   a - mould-'ring   in   the   grave,
The   stars   of   hea - ven   are   look - ing   kind - ly   down,
gone   to   be   a   sol - dier   in   the   ar - my   of   the   Lord,   He's
John   Brown   died   that   the   slave   might   be   free,
John   Brown's   knap - sack   is   strapped   to   his   back,
His   pet   lambs   will   meet   on   the   way,
They   will   hang   Jeff   Da - vis   on   a   sour   ap - ple   tree,

G   **B⁷**   **Em**

/	/	/	/	/	/	/	/

John   Brown's   bo - dy   lies   a - mould-'ring   in   the   grave,   But   his
The   stars   of   hea - ven   are   look - ing   kind - ly   down,   On   the
gone   to   be   a   sol - dier   in   the   ar - my   of   the   Lord,   His
John   Brown   died   that   the   slave   might   be   free,   But   his
John   Brown's   knap - sack   is   strapped   to   his   back,   His
His   pet   lambs   will   meet   on   the   way,   And
They   will   hang   Jeff   Da - vis   on   a   sour   ap - ple   tree,   As

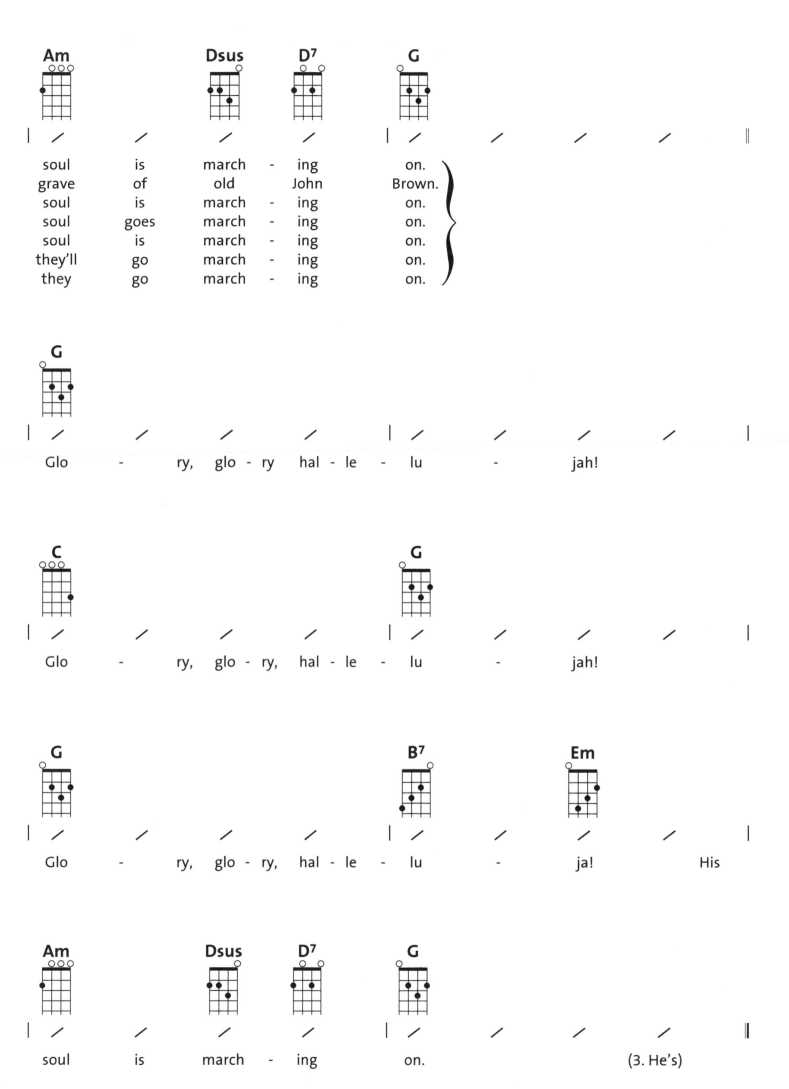

soul   is   march - ing   on.
grave   of   old   John   Brown.
soul   is   march - ing   on.
soul   goes   march - ing   on.
soul   is   march - ing   on.
they'll   go   march - ing   on.
they   go   march - ing   on.

Glo - ry, glo - ry hal - le - lu - jah!

Glo - ry, glo - ry, hal - le - lu - jah!

Glo - ry, glo - ry, hal - le - lu - ja!   His

soul   is   march - ing   on.   (3. He's)

29

joshua (fit the battle of jericho)

African-American spiritual

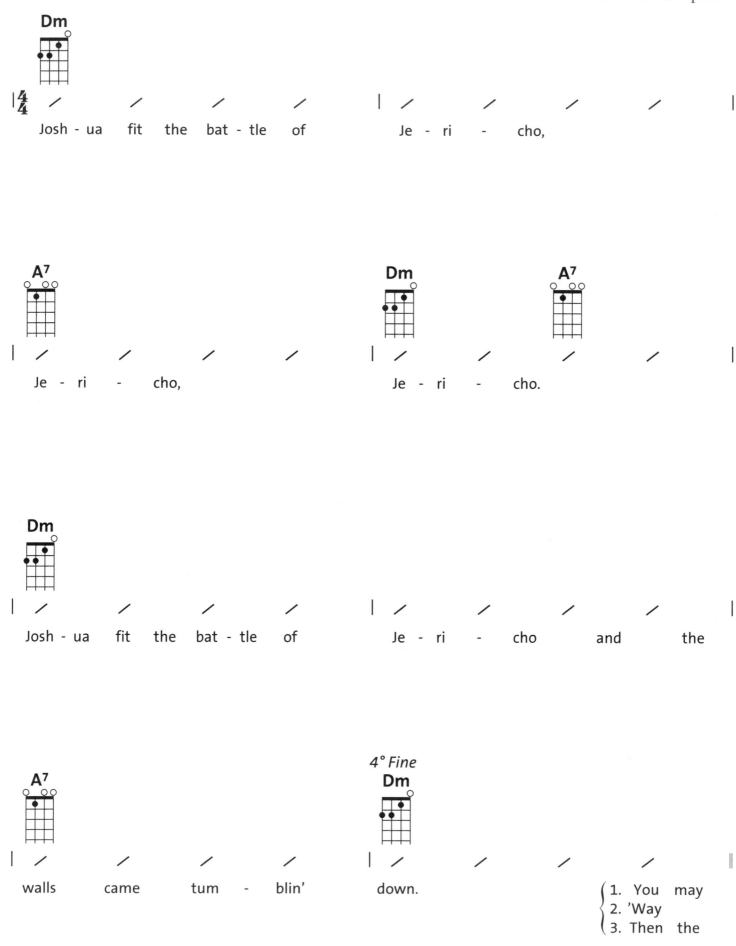

Dm
Josh - ua fit the bat - tle of Je - ri - cho,

A⁷
Je - ri - cho,

Dm **A⁷**
Je - ri - cho.

Dm
Josh - ua fit the bat - tle of Je - ri - cho and the

A⁷ *4° Fine* **Dm**
walls came tum - blin' down.

{ 1. You may
{ 2. 'Way
{ 3. Then the

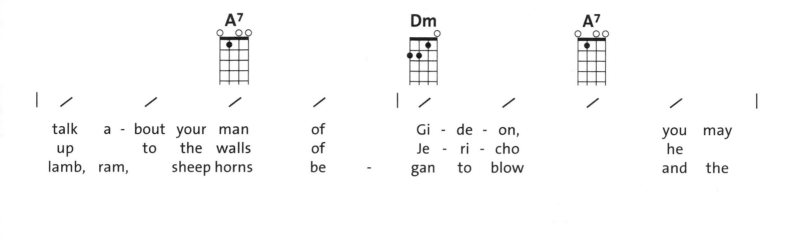

A7				**Dm**		**A7**	

talk   a - bout your man   of   Gi - de - on,   you may
up   to   the walls   of   Je - ri - cho   he
lamb, ram,   sheep horns be -   gan to blow   and the

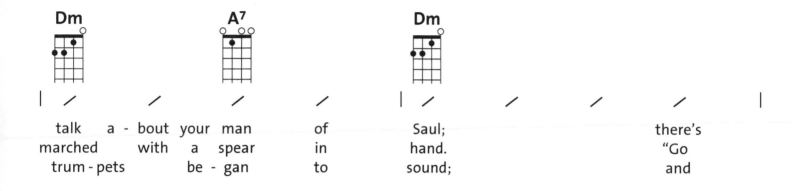

Dm		**A7**		**Dm**			

talk   a - bout your man   of   Saul;   there's
marched with a spear   in   hand.   "Go
trum - pets   be - gan   to   sound;   and

		A7		**Dm**			

none   like   good   old   Josh - u - a   at   the
blow   the   ram's   horn,"   Josh - ua cried, "'cause the
Josh - ua com - mand - ed the   child - ren to shout   and   the

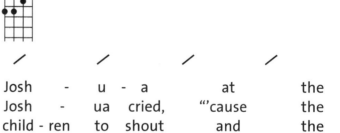

Play 4 times

A7				**Dm**			

bat - tle   of   Je - ri - cho.
bat - tle   is   in   my   hands."
walls   came   tum - blin'   down.

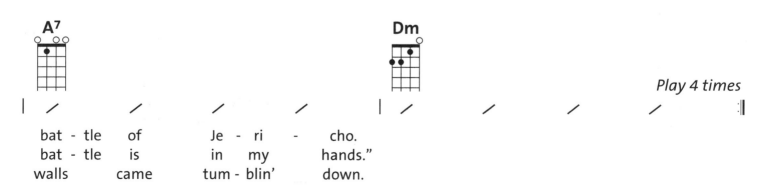

hush, little baby

American folksong

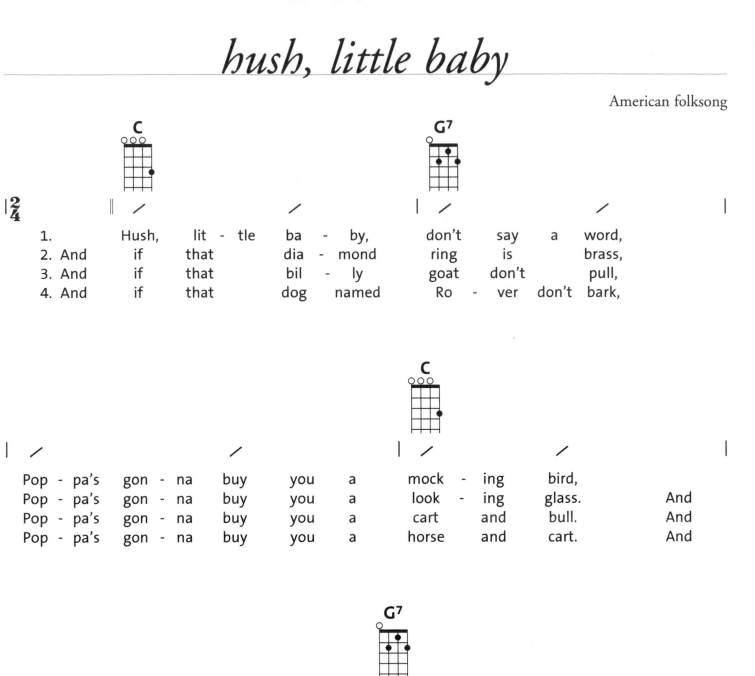

1.	Hush,	lit - tle	ba - by,	don't	say a	word,
2. And	if	that	dia - mond	ring	is	brass,
3. And	if	that	bil - ly	goat	don't	pull,
4. And	if	that	dog named	Ro - ver	don't bark,

Pop - pa's gon - na buy you a mock - ing bird,
Pop - pa's gon - na buy you a look - ing glass. And
Pop - pa's gon - na buy you a cart and bull. And
Pop - pa's gon - na buy you a horse and cart. And

If that mock - ing bird don't sing
if that look - ing glass gets broke,
if that cart and bull turn ov - er
if that horse and cart fall down,

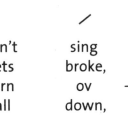

Pop - pa's gon - na buy you a dia - mond ring.
Pop - pa's gon - na buy you a bil - ly goat.
Pop - pa's gon - na buy you a dog named Ro - ver.
you'll still be the sweet - est lit - tle ba - by in town.

just a closer walk with thee

American

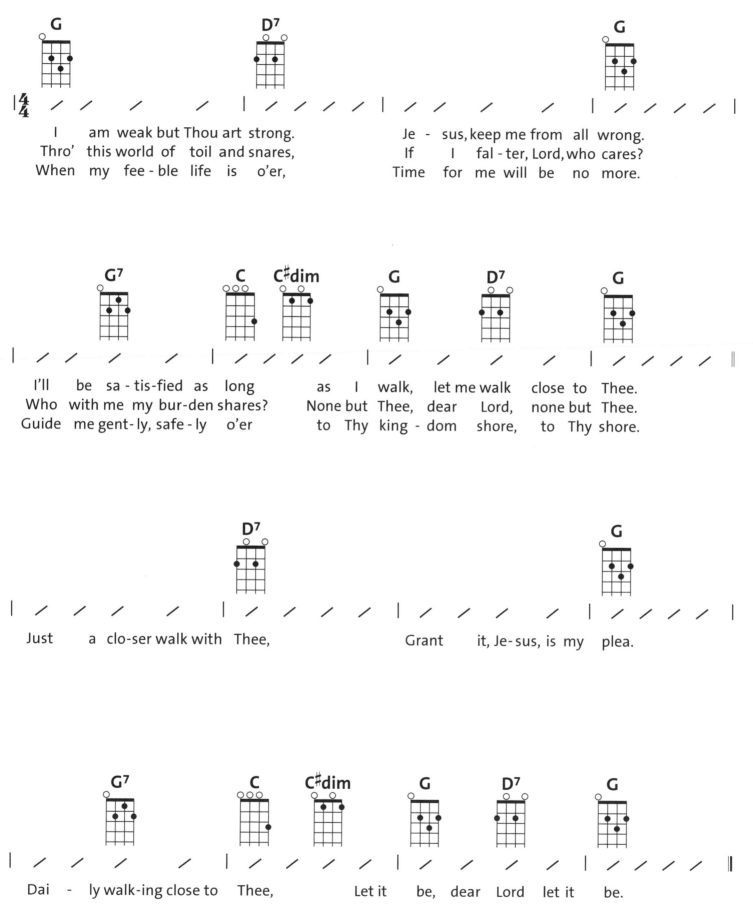

G   D⁷   G

I am weak but Thou art strong. Je - sus, keep me from all wrong.
Thro' this world of toil and snares, If I fal - ter, Lord, who cares?
When my fee - ble life is o'er, Time for me will be no more.

G⁷   C   C♯dim   G   D⁷   G

I'll be sa - tis-fied as long as I walk, let me walk close to Thee.
Who with me my bur-den shares? None but Thee, dear Lord, none but Thee.
Guide me gent - ly, safe - ly o'er to Thy king - dom shore, to Thy shore.

D⁷   G

Just a clo-ser walk with Thee, Grant it, Je-sus, is my plea.

G⁷   C   C♯dim   G   D⁷   G

Dai - ly walk-ing close to Thee, Let it be, dear Lord let it be.

the lincolnshire poacher

English folksong

G   **Em**   **D**   **G**

6/8

1. When I was bound ap - pren - tice in
2. As me and my com - pa - nions were
3. As me and my com - pa - nions were
4. I threw him on my shoul - der and
5. Suc - cess to ev - 'ry gen - tle - man that

D   **G**

fa - mous Lin - coln - shire, full
set - ting of a snare, 'twas
set - ting four or five and
then we trudged home. We
lives in Lin - coln - shire, suc -

well I served my mas - ter for
then we spied the game - keep - er, for
tak - ing on 'em up a - gain, we
took him to a neigh - bour's house and
-cess to ev - 'ry poach - er that

A⁷   **D**

more than se - ven years 'till
him we did not care. For
caught a hare a - live. We
sold him for a crown. We
wants to sell a hare. Bad

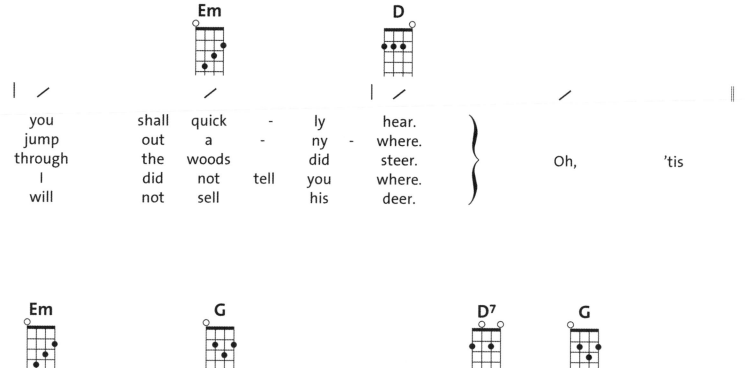

G

| / | / | | / | / | |

I took up to poach - ing, as
we can wre - stle and fight, my boys, and
took a hare a - live, my boys, and
sold him for a crown, my boys, but
luck to ev - 'ry game - keep - er that

Em **D**

| / | / | | / | / | ‖

you shall quick - ly hear.
jump out a - ny - where.
through the woods did steer.
I did not tell you where.
will not sell his deer.

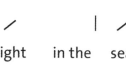 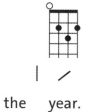 Oh, 'tis

Em **G** **D⁷** **G**

| / / | / / | / / | / / |

my de-light of a shi - ny night in the sea - son of the year. Oh, 'tis

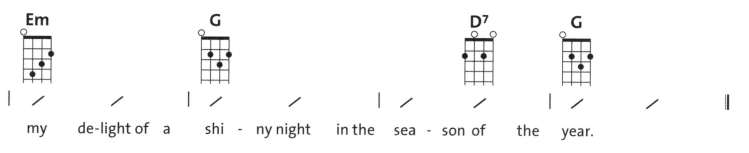

Em **G** **D⁷** **G**

| / / | / / | / / | / / ‖

my de-light of a shi - ny night in the sea - son of the year.

lavender's blue

American folksong

D

| 3/4 | / | / | / | | / | / | / | |

1. La - ven - der's   blue,   dil - ly,   dil - ly,
2. Call   up   your   men,   dil - ly,   dil - ly,
3. Some   to   make   hay,   dil - ly,   dil - ly,
4. La - ven - der's   green,   dil - ly,   dil - ly,

G

La - ven - der's   green,
Set   them   to   work,
Some   to   cut   corn,
La - ven - der's   blue,

D

When   I   am   king,   dil - ly,   dil - ly,
Some   to   the   plough,   dil - ly,   dil - ly,
While   you   and   I,   dil - ly,   dil - ly,
If   you   love   me,   dil - ly,   dil - ly,

A⁷   **D**

You   shall   be   queen.
Some   to   the   cart.
Keep   our - selves   warm.
I   will   love   you.

mama don't 'low

American folksong

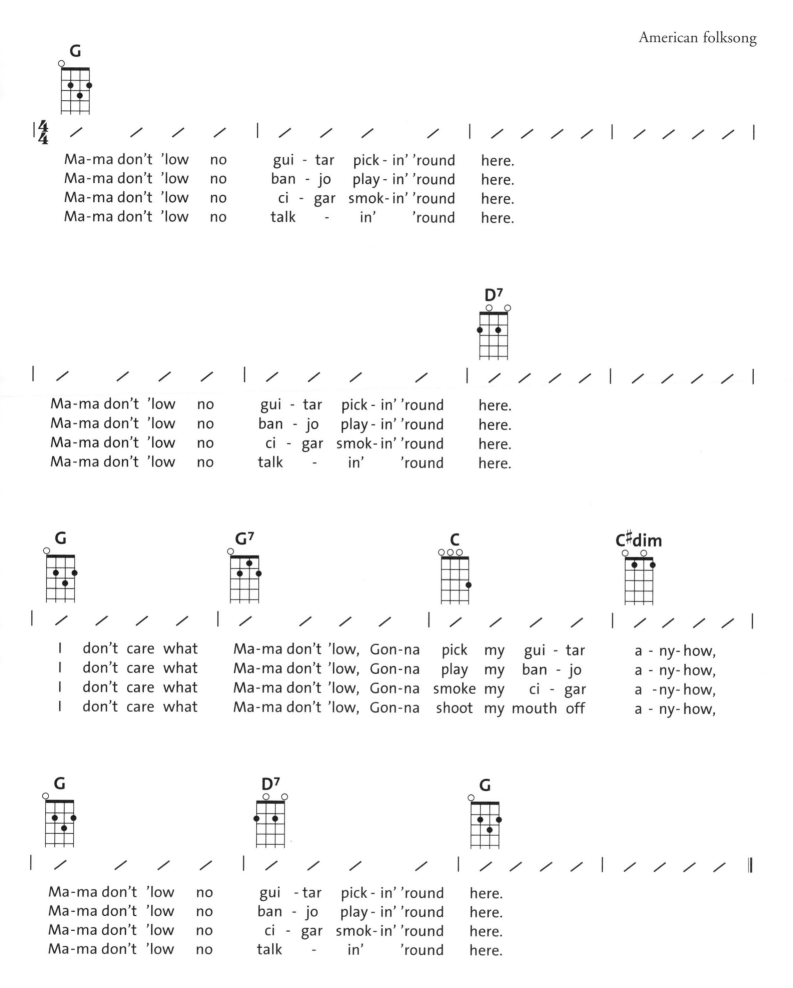

michael finnegan

American folksong

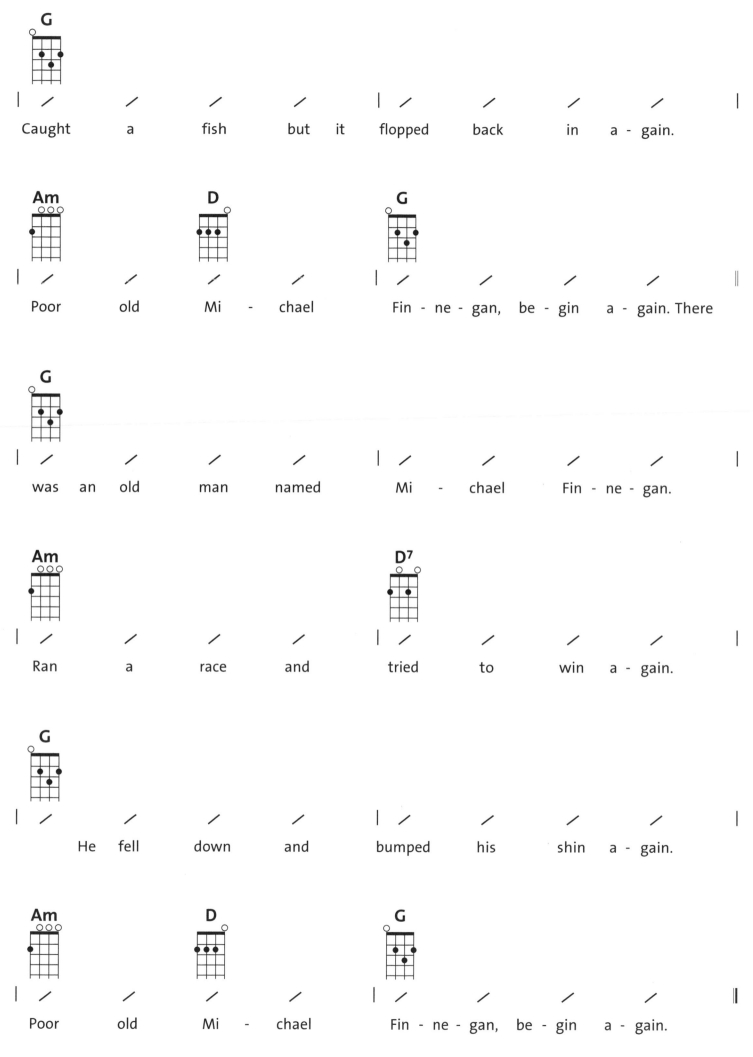

G

Caught a fish but it flopped back in a - gain.

Am **D** **G**

Poor old Mi - chael Fin - ne - gan, be - gin a - gain. There

G

was an old man named Mi - chael Fin - ne - gan.

Am **D⁷**

Ran a race and tried to win a - gain.

G

He fell down and bumped his shin a - gain.

Am **D** **G**

Poor old Mi - chael Fin - ne - gan, be - gin a - gain.

my bonnie lies over the ocean

Scottish folksong

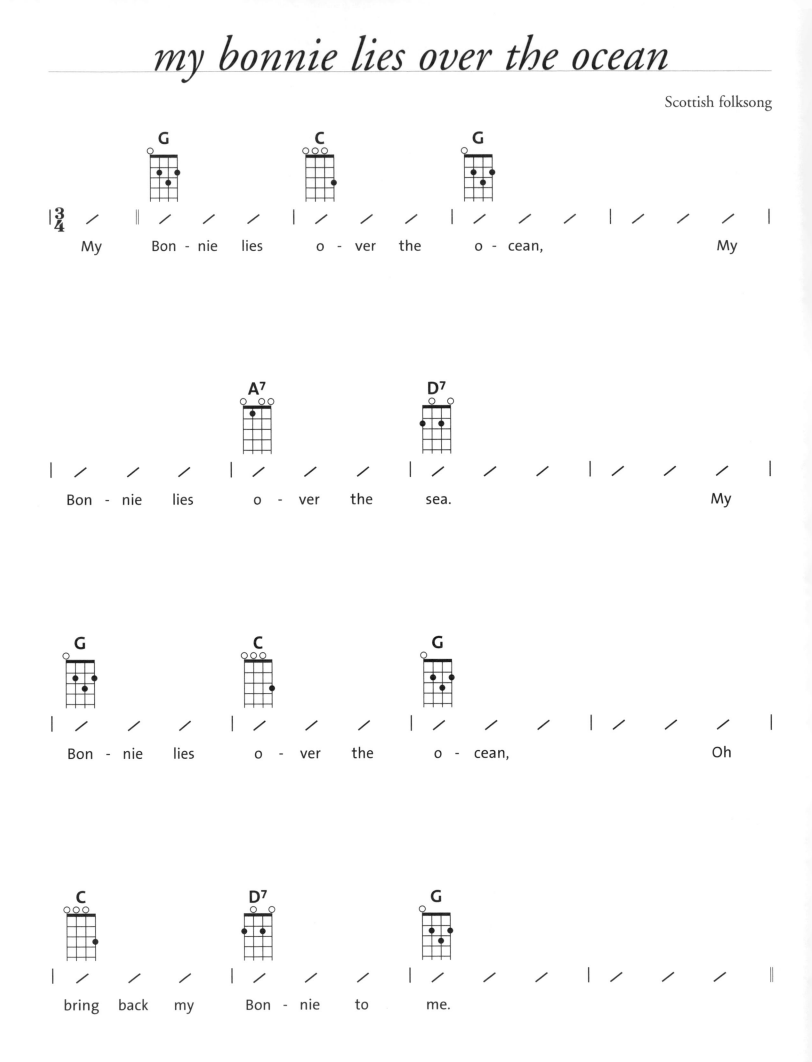

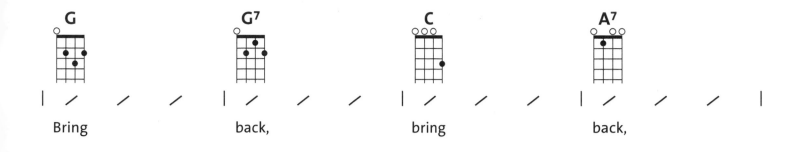

Bring   back,   bring   back,

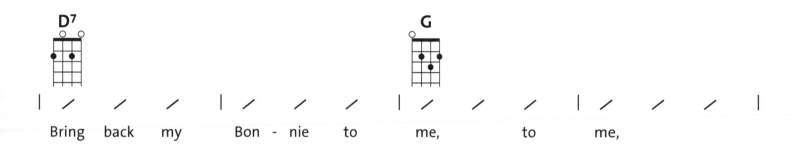

Bring   back   my   Bon - nie   to   me,   to   me,

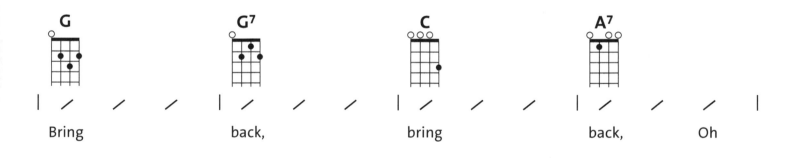

Bring   back,   bring   back,   Oh

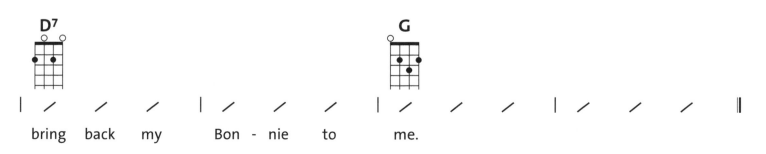

bring   back   my   Bon - nie   to   me.

molly malone

Irish folksong

nobody knows the trouble i've seen

African-American spiritual

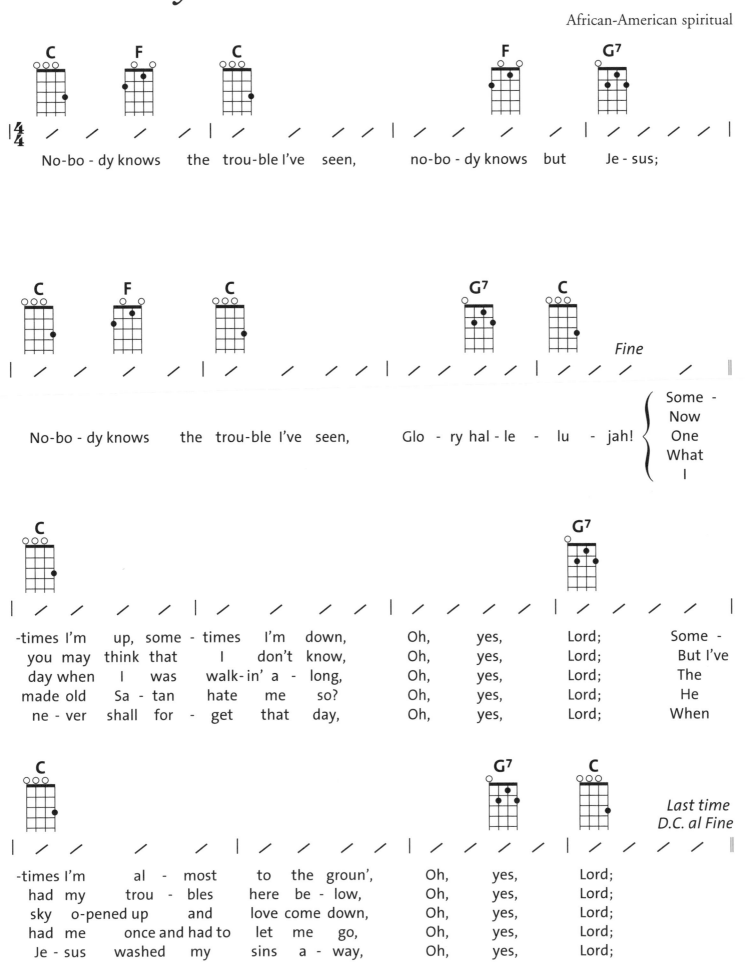

oh dear! what can the matter be?

American folksong

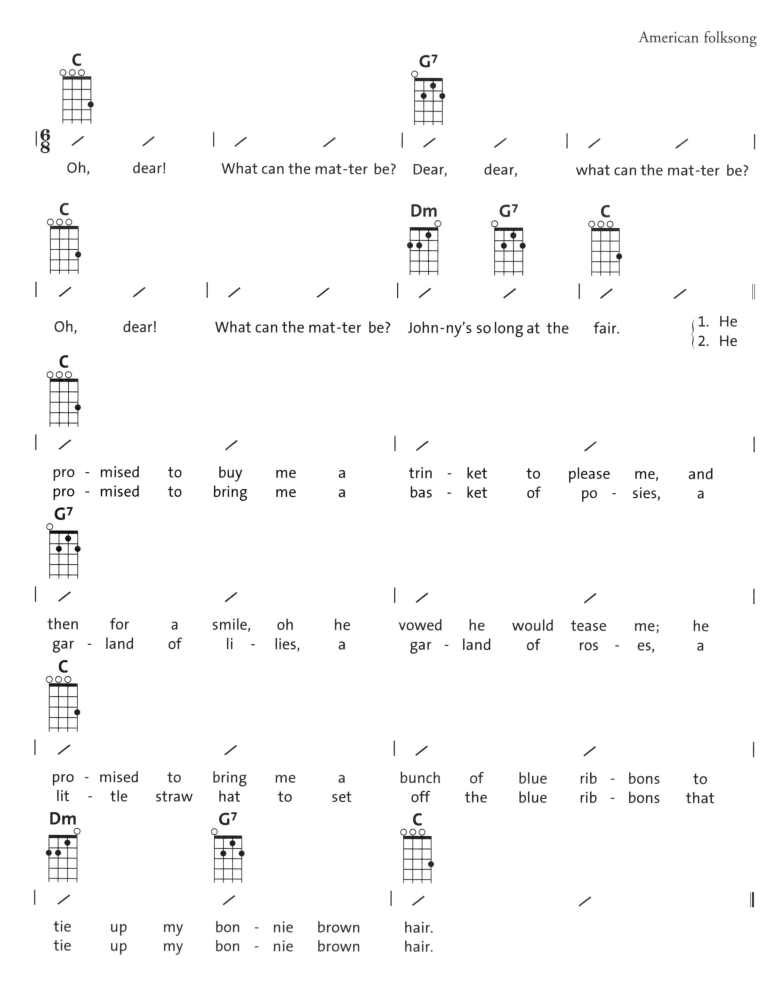

oh! susanna

Words and Music by Stephen C. Foster

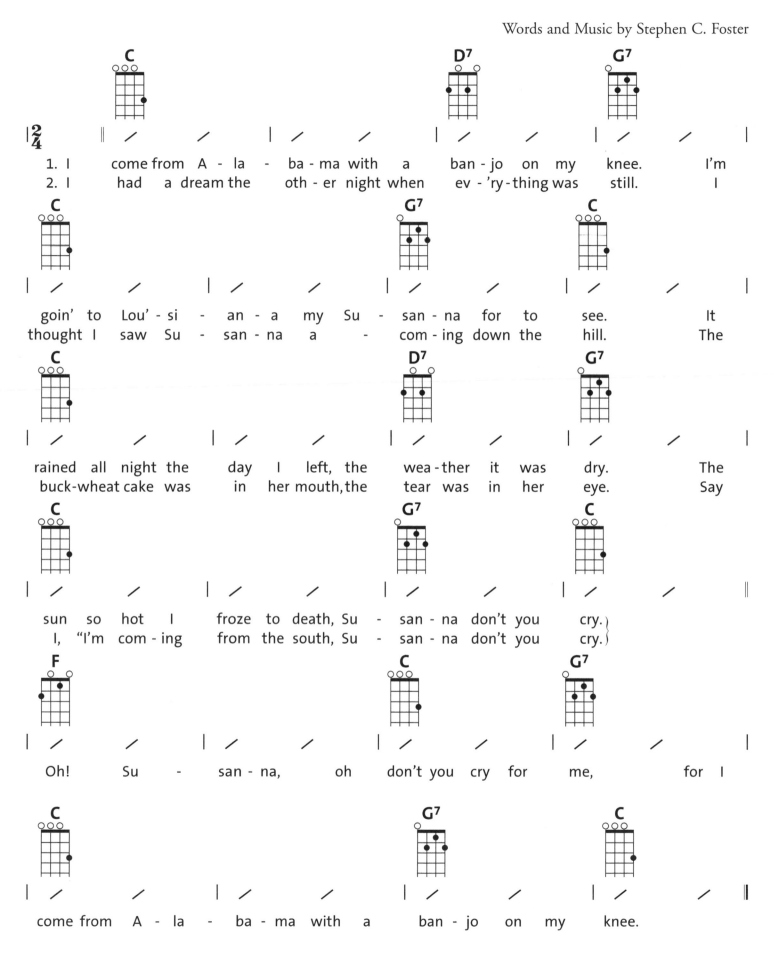

1. I come from A - la - ba - ma with a ban - jo on my knee. I'm
2. I had a dream the oth - er night when ev - 'ry - thing was still. I

goin' to Lou' - si - an - a my Su - san - na for to see. It
thought I saw Su - san - na a - com - ing down the hill. The

rained all night the day I left, the wea - ther it was dry. The
buck-wheat cake was in her mouth, the tear was in her eye. Say

sun so hot I froze to death, Su - san - na don't you cry.
I, "I'm com - ing from the south, Su - san - na don't you cry.

Oh! Su - san - na, oh don't you cry for me, for I

come from A - la - ba - ma with a ban - jo on my knee.

on top of old smoky

American folksong

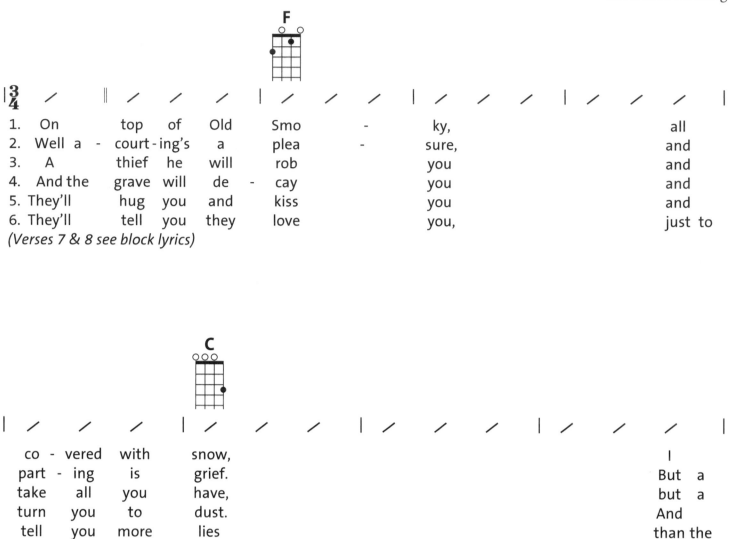

1. On   top   of   Old   Smo   -   ky,   all
2. Well a - court-ing's   a   plea   -   sure,   and
3. A   thief he   will rob   you   and
4. And the   grave will de - cay   you   and
5. They'll   hug   you and   kiss   you   and
6. They'll   tell   you they love   you,   just to

(Verses 7 & 8 see block lyrics)

co - vered with   snow,   I
part - ing   is   grief.   But a
take   all   you   have,   but a
turn   you   to   dust.   And
tell   you   more lies   than the
give   your   heart ease.   But the

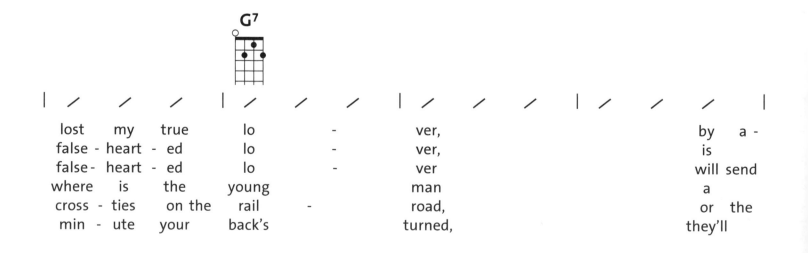

lost   my   true   lo   -   ver,   by a -
false - heart - ed   lo   -   ver,   is
false - heart - ed   lo   -   ver   will send
where   is   the   young   man   a
cross - ties on the rail   -   road,   or the
min - ute   your   back's   turned,   they'll

| / | / | / | | / | / | / | | / | / | / | | / | / | / | ‖

court - in'   too   slow.
worse   than   a   thief.
you   to   your   grave.
poor   girl   can   trust?
stars   in   the   skies.
court   whom   they   please.

7. So come all you young maidens
   And listen to me.
   Never place your affection
   On a green willow tree.

8. For the leaves they will wither
   And the roots they will die,
   And your true love will leave you
   And you'll never know why.

old macdonald had a farm

English folksong

G   **C**   **G**   **D⁷**   **G**

1. Old Mac - Do - nald   had a farm   E - I - E - I - O!   And
(Verses 2-10 see block lyrics)

C   **G**   **D⁷**   **G**

on this farm he   had a duck,   E - I - E - I - O!   With a

quack - quack here,   and a   quack - quack   there,

Here a quack,   there a quack,   Ev - 'ry - where a quack,   quack.

C   **G**   **D⁷**   **G**

Old Mac - Do - nald   had a farm,   E - I - E - I - O!

2. Old MacDonald had a farm,
E - I - E - I - O!
And on this farm he had a chick,
E - I - E - I - O!
With a chick, chick here
And a chick, chick there,
Here a chick, there a chick,
Everywhere a chick, chick
Old Mac-Do-nald had a farm,
E - I - E - I - O!

3. Cow – moo, moo
4. Dogs – bow, bow
5. Pigs – oink, oink
6. Rooster – cock-a-doodle, cock-a-doodle
7. Turkey – gobble, gobble
8. Cat – meow, meow
9. Horse – neigh, neigh
10. Donkey – hee-haw, hee-haw

polly put the kettle on

American children's song

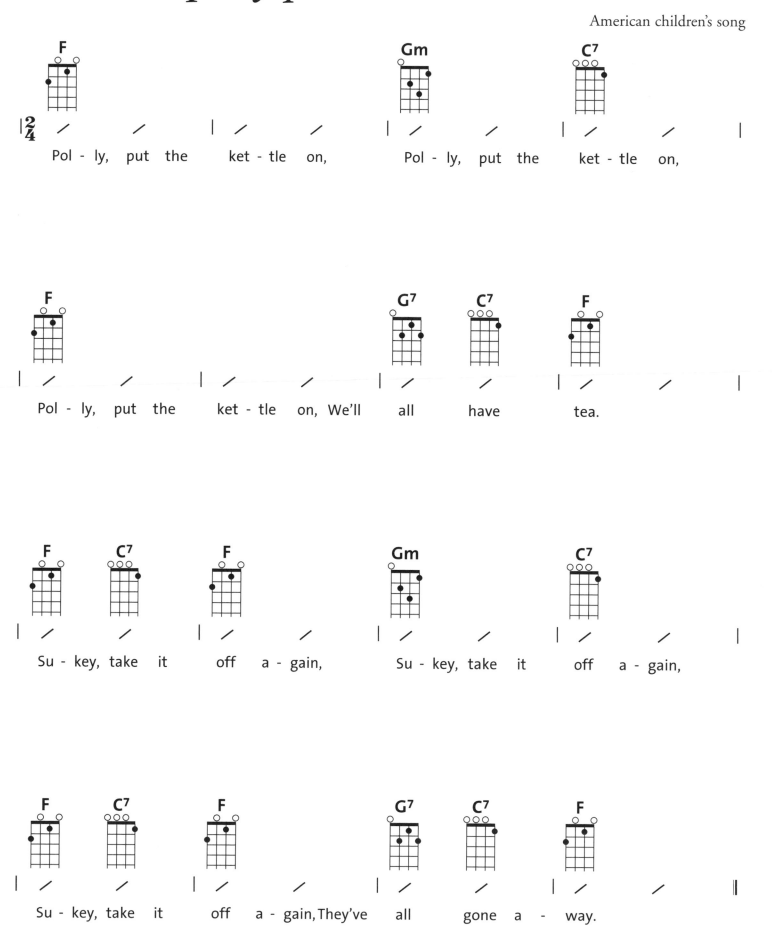

pop goes the weasel

American children's song

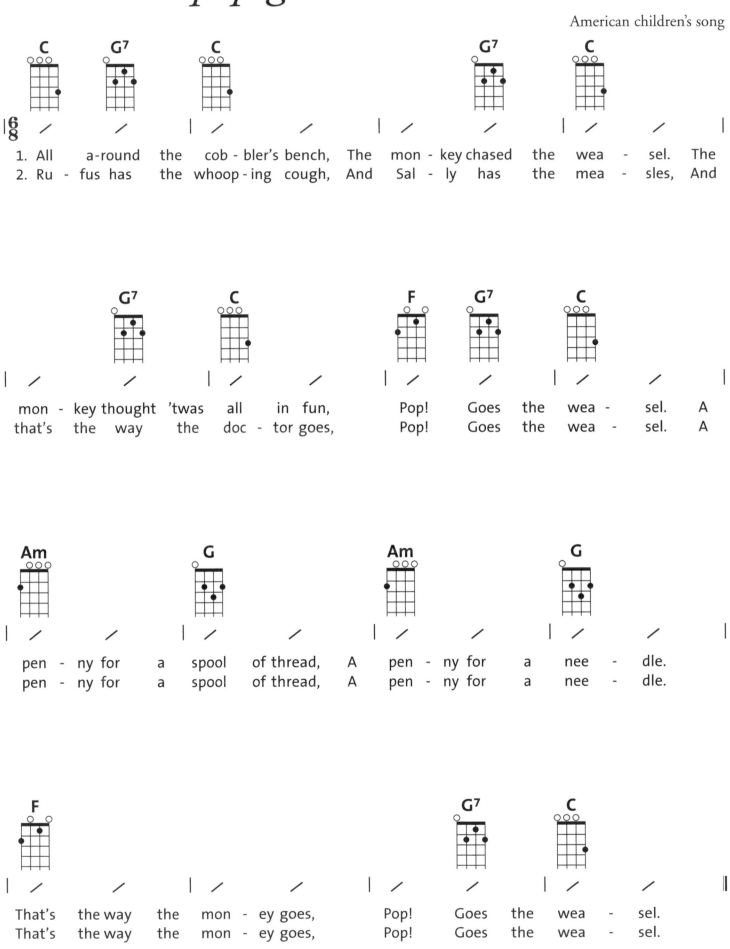

1. All a-round the cob-bler's bench, The mon-key chased the wea - sel. The
2. Ru - fus has the whoop-ing cough, And Sal - ly has the mea - sles, And

mon - key thought 'twas all in fun, Pop! Goes the wea - sel. A
that's the way the doc - tor goes, Pop! Goes the wea - sel. A

pen - ny for a spool of thread, A pen - ny for a nee - dle.
pen - ny for a spool of thread, A pen - ny for a nee - dle.

That's the way the mon - ey goes, Pop! Goes the wea - sel.
That's the way the mon - ey goes, Pop! Goes the wea - sel.

rivers of babylon

Jamaican spiritual

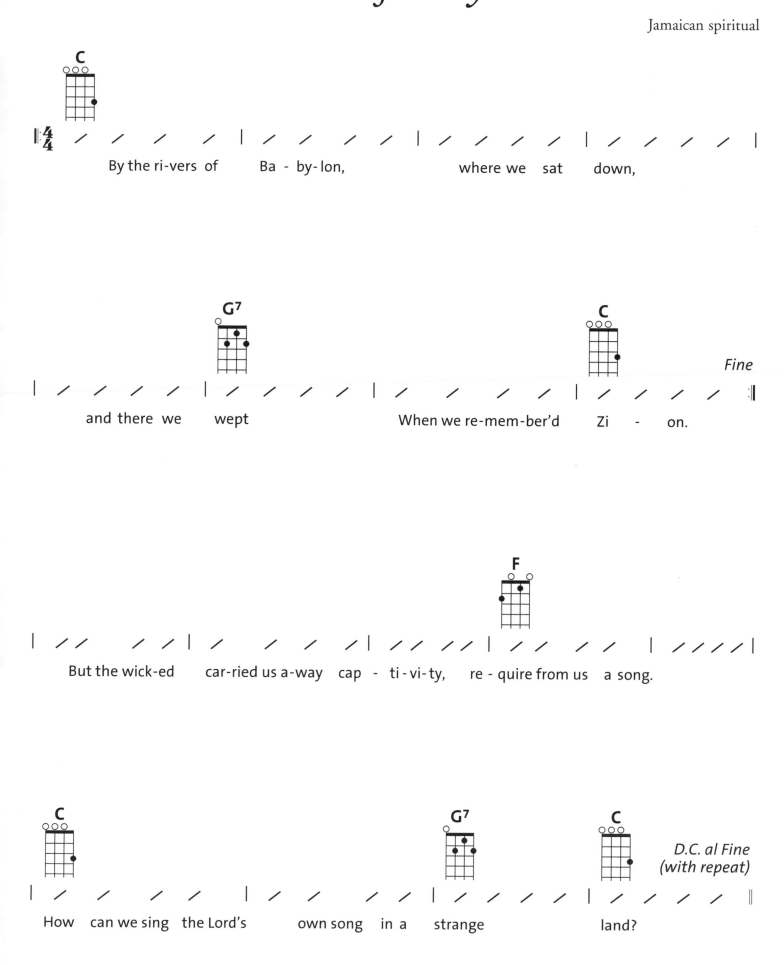

By the ri-vers of   Ba - by-lon,   where we sat   down,

and there we   wept   When we re-mem-ber'd   Zi - on.   *Fine*

But the wick-ed   car-ried us a-way cap - ti-vi-ty,   re - quire from us   a song.

How   can we sing the Lord's   own song in a   strange   land?

D.C. al Fine
(with repeat)

santa lucia

Neapolitan folksong

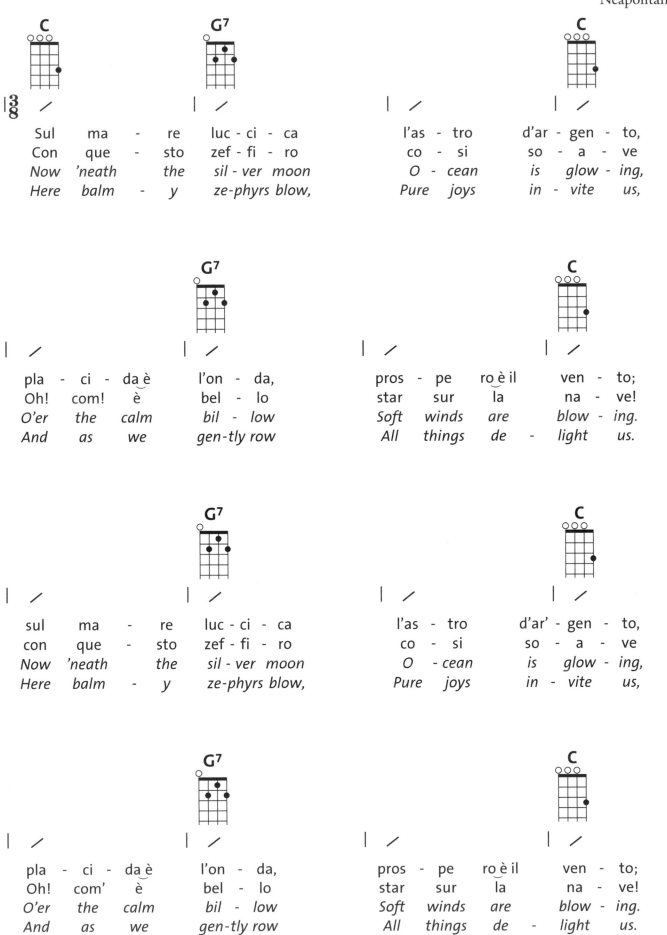

Sul ma - re luc - ci - ca l'as - tro d'ar - gen - to,
Con que - sto zef - fi - ro co - si so - a - ve
Now 'neath the sil - ver moon O - cean is glow - ing,
Here balm - y ze-phyrs blow, Pure joys in - vite us,

pla - ci - da è l'on - da, pros - pe ro è il ven - to;
Oh! com! è bel - lo star sur la na - ve!
O'er the calm bil - low Soft winds are blow - ing.
And as we gen-tly row All things de - light us.

sul ma - re luc - ci - ca l'as - tro d'ar' - gen - to,
con que - sto zef - fi - ro co - si so - a - ve
Now 'neath the sil - ver moon O - cean is glow - ing,
Here balm - y ze-phyrs blow, Pure joys in - vite us,

pla - ci - da è l'on - da, pros - pe ro è il ven - to;
Oh! com' è bel - lo star sur la na - ve!
O'er the calm bil - low Soft winds are blow - ing.
And as we gen-tly row All things de - light us.

F⁶   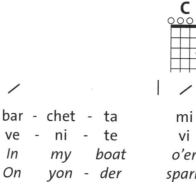 **C**

| / | | / | | / | | / | |

ve - ni - te al — l'a - gi - le   bar - chet - ta   mi - a...
su pas - sag - gie - ri,   ve - ni - te   vi - a!
Who then will — sail with me   In my boat   o'er the sea?
Who will em - bark with me   On yon - der   spark-ling sea?

G⁷   **C**

| / | | / | | / | | / | |

San - ta Lu - ci - a!   San - ta Lu - ci - a!
San - ta Lu - ci - a!   San - ta Lu - ci - a!
San - ta Lu - ci - a!   *San - ta Lu - ci - a!*
San - ta Lu - ci - a!   *San - ta Lu - ci - a!*

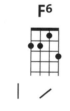 **F⁶**   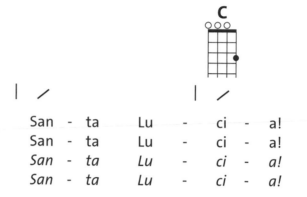 **C**

| / | | / | | / | | / | |

ve - ni - te al — l'a - gi - le   bar - chet - ta   mi - a...
su pas - sag - gie - ri,   ve - ni - te   vi - a!
Who then will — sail with me   In my boat   o'er the sea?
Who will em - bark with me   On yon - der   spark-ling sea?

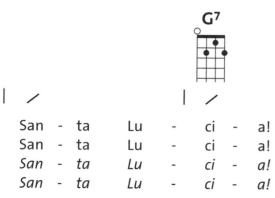 **G⁷**   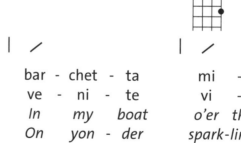 **C**

| / | | / | | / | | / | ||

San - ta Lu - ci - a!   San - ta Lu - ci - a!
San - ta Lu - ci - a!   San - ta Lu - ci - a!
San - ta Lu - ci - a!   *San - ta Lu - ci - a!*
San - ta Lu - ci - a!   *San - ta Lu - ci - a!*

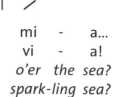

scarborough fair

English folksong

Am   **G**   **Am**

6/8				
1. Are	you	go - ing	to	Scar - bo-rough Fair?
2. Tell	her	to make	me a	cam - bric shirt,
3. Tell	her	to wash	in	yon - der well,
4. Tell	her	to plough	me an	a - cre of land,
5. Tell	her	to plough	it with	one ram's horn,
6. Tell	her	to reap	it with a	sick - le of lea - ther,
7. Tell	her	to ga - ther	it all	in a sack,

C   **Am**   **C**   **D**   **Am**

Pars - ley, sage,	rose - ma - ry and thyme,	Re -
Pars - ley, sage,	rose - ma - ry and thyme,	With -
Pars - ley, sage,	rose - ma - ry and thyme,	Where
Pars - ley, sage,	rose - ma - ry and thyme,	Be -
Pars - ley, sage,	rose - ma - ry and thyme,	And
Pars - ley, sage,	rose - ma - ry and thyme,	And
Pars - ley, sage,	rose - ma - ry and thyme,	And

C   **G**

-mem - ber me to a	bon - ny lass there,	for
- out a - ny nee - dle or	thread work'd in it,	and
wa - ter ne'er sprung nor a	drop of rain fell	and
tween the sea and the	salt sea strand,	and
sow it all ov - er with	one pep - per - corn	and
tie it all up with a	tom - tit's fea - ther,	and
car - ry it home on a	but - ter - fly's back	and

Am   **G**   3/8   6/8   **Am**

once	she was	a true	lov - er	of	mine.
she	shall be	a true	lov - er	of	mine.
she	shall be	a true	lov - er	of	mine.
she	shall be	a true	lov - er	of	mine.
she	shall be	a true	lov - er	of	mine.
she	shall be	a true	lov - er	of	mine.
she	shall be	a true	lov - er	of	mine.

skye boat song

Scottish sea shanty

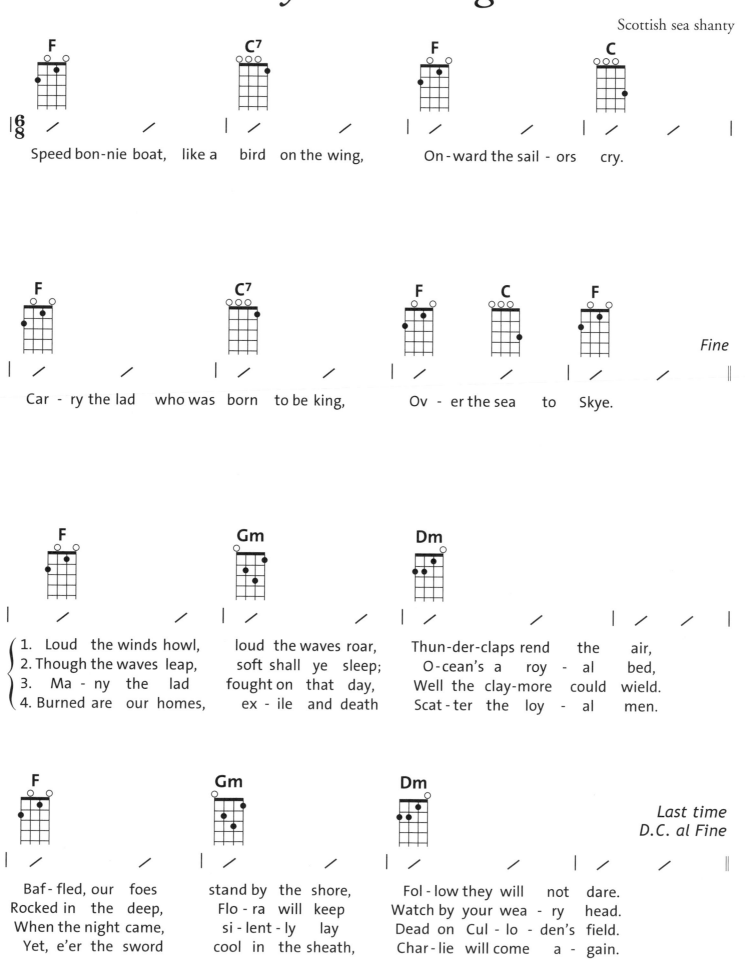

F **C⁷** **F** **C**

Speed bon-nie boat, like a bird on the wing, On-ward the sail - ors cry.

F **C⁷** **F** **C** **F**

Fine

Car - ry the lad who was born to be king, Ov - er the sea to Skye.

F **Gm** **Dm**

1. Loud the winds howl, loud the waves roar, Thun-der-claps rend the air,
2. Though the waves leap, soft shall ye sleep; O-cean's a roy - al bed,
3. Ma - ny the lad fought on that day, Well the clay-more could wield.
4. Burned are our homes, ex - ile and death Scat-ter the loy - al men.

F **Gm** **Dm**

Last time
D.C. al Fine

Baf-fled, our foes stand by the shore, Fol - low they will not dare.
Rocked in the deep, Flo - ra will keep Watch by your wea - ry head.
When the night came, si - lent-ly lay Dead on Cul - lo - den's field.
Yet, e'er the sword cool in the sheath, Char - lie will come a - gain.

the streets of laredo

19th Century American

1. As I was a - walk - in' the streets of La - re - do, As
2. "I see by your out - fit that you are a cow - boy," these
3. "It was once in the sad - dle I used to go dash - ing, once
4. "Get six - teen gam - blers to car - ry my cof - fin, let
5. "Oh bang the drum slow - ly and play the fife low - ly,

I walked out in La - re - do one day, I
words he did say as I bold - ly walked by. "Come
in the sad - dle I used to go gay. First
six jol - ly cow - boys come sing me a song. Take
play the dead march as you car-ry me a - long. Put

spied a young cow - boy all wrapped in white li - nen, All
sit down be - side me and hear my sad sto - ry, I'm
down to Ro - sie's and then to the card house. Got
me to the grave - yard and lay the sod o'er me, for
bunch - es of ros - es all ov - er my cof - fin,

wrapped in white li - nen, and cold as the clay."
shot in the breast and I know I must die."
shot in the breast and I'm dy - ing to - day."
I'm a young cow - boy and I know I've done wrong."
ros - es to dead - en the clods as they fall."

there's a hole in my bucket

English folksong

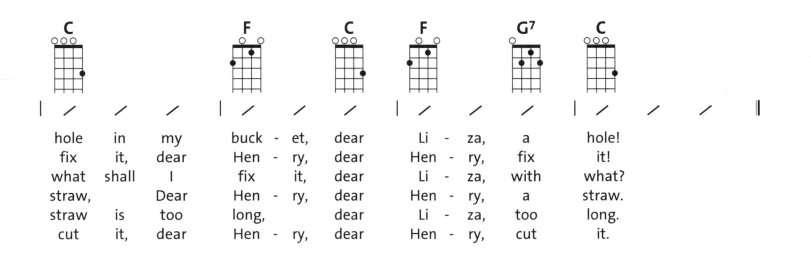

3/4

1. There's a	hole	in	my	buck - et,	dear Li - za, dear Li - za. There's a
2. Well	fix	it,	dear	Hen - ry,	dear Hen - ry, dear Hen - ry. Well,
3. With	what	shall	I	fix it,	dear Li - za, dear Li - za? With
4. With a	straw,	Dear	Hen - ry,	dear Hen - ry,	dear Hen - ry. With a
5. But the	straw	is	too	long,	dear Li - za, dear Li - za. But the
6. Then	cut	it,	dear	Hen - ry,	dear Hen - ry, dear Hen - ry. Then

(Verses 7-19 see block lyrics)

hole	in	my	buck - et,	dear Li - za,	a hole!
fix	it,	dear	Hen - ry,	dear Hen - ry,	fix it!
what	shall	I	fix it,	dear Li - za,	with what?
straw,		Dear	Hen - ry,	dear Hen - ry,	a straw.
straw	is	too	long,	dear Li - za,	too long.
cut	it,	dear	Hen - ry,	dear Hen - ry,	cut it.

7. With what shall I cut it, dear Liza, *etc.*
8. With a knife, dear Henry, *etc.*
9. But the knife is too dull, dear Liza, *etc.*
10. Then sharpen it, dear Henry, *etc.*
11. With what shall I sharpen it, dear Liza, *etc.*
12. With a stone, dear Henry, *etc.*
13. But the stone is too dry, dear Liza, *etc.*
14. Then wet it, dear Henry, *etc.*
15. With what shall I wet it, dear Liza, *etc.*
16. With water, dear Henry, *etc.*
17. In what shall I carry it, dear Liza, *etc.*
18. In a bucket, dear Henry, *etc.*
19. There's a hole in my bucket, dear Liza, *etc.*

when johnny comes marching home

Words and Music by Louis Lambert

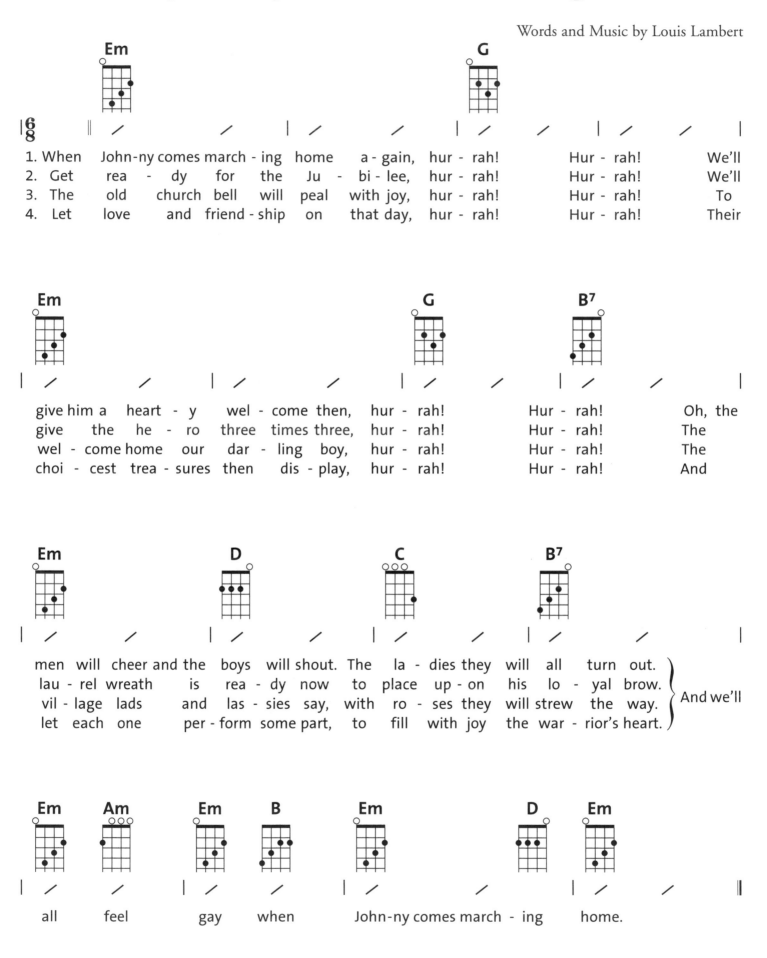

will the circle be unbroken

Words by Ada R. Habershon
Music by Charles H. Gabriel

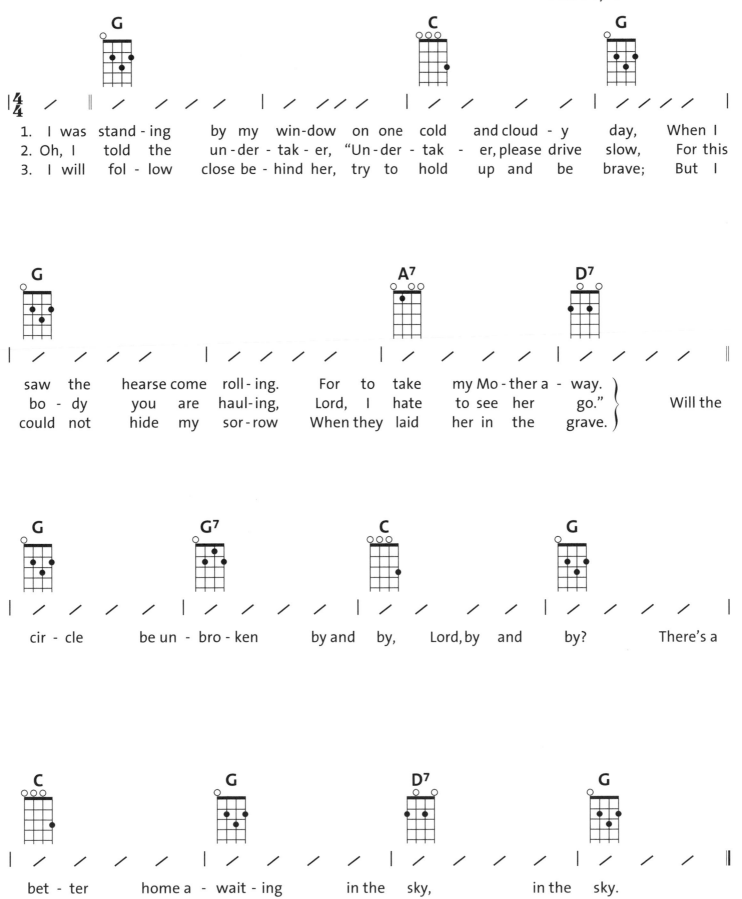

1. I was stand-ing by my win-dow on one cold and cloud-y day, When I
2. Oh, I told the un-der-tak-er, "Un-der-tak-er, please drive slow, For this
3. I will fol-low close be-hind her, try to hold up and be brave; But I

saw the hearse come roll-ing. For to take my Mo-ther a-way.
bo-dy you are haul-ing, Lord, I hate to see her go."
could not hide my sor-row When they laid her in the grave.

Will the

cir-cle be un-bro-ken by and by, Lord, by and by? There's a

bet-ter home a-wait-ing in the sky, in the sky.

the yellow rose of texas

Words and Music by J. K., 1858

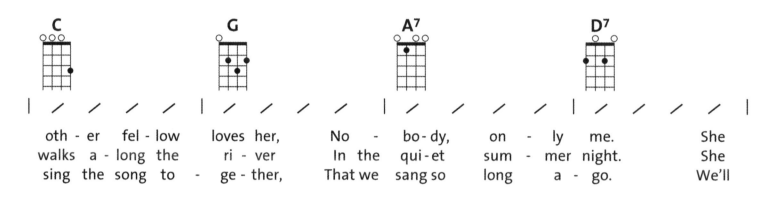

1. There's a   yel-low rose in   Tex-as   That   I am goin' to see,   No
2. Where the   Ri-o Grande is   flow-ing   And the star-ry skies   are bright,   She
3. Oh,   now I'm goin' to   find her   For my   heart is   full   of woe,   And we'll

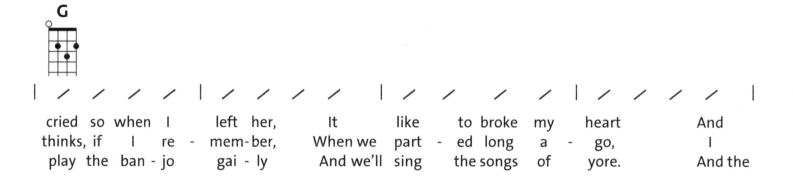

oth-er fel-low   loves her,   No -   bo-dy,   on - ly me.   She
walks a-long the   ri - ver   In the qui-et   sum - mer night.   She
sing the song to - ge-ther,   That we sang so   long   a - go.   We'll

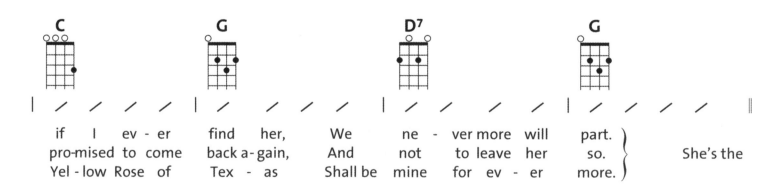

cried so when I   left her,   It   like   to broke my   heart   And
thinks, if I re - mem-ber,   When we part - ed long a - go,   I
play the ban-jo   gai-ly   And we'll sing the songs of   yore.   And the

if   I ev - er   find her,   We   ne - ver more will   part.)
pro-mised to come   back a-gain, And   not   to leave her   so. }   She's the
Yel-low Rose of   Tex - as   Shall be mine for ev - er   more.)

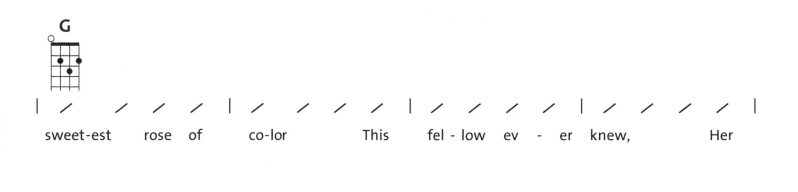

G

| / / / / | / / / / | / / / / | / / / / |

sweet-est   rose of   co-lor   This   fel - low ev - er knew,   Her

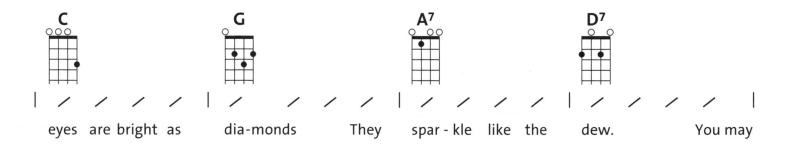

C   **G**   **A⁷**   **D⁷**

| / / / / | / / / / | / / / / | / / / / |

eyes are bright as   dia-monds   They   spar - kle like the   dew.   You may

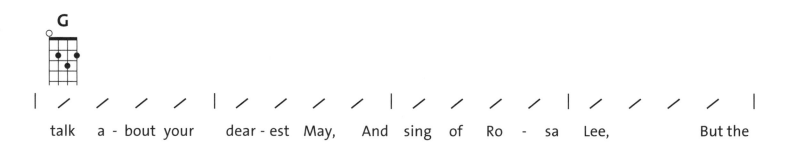

G

| / / / / | / / / / | / / / / | / / / / |

talk a - bout your   dear - est May,   And sing of Ro - sa Lee,   But the

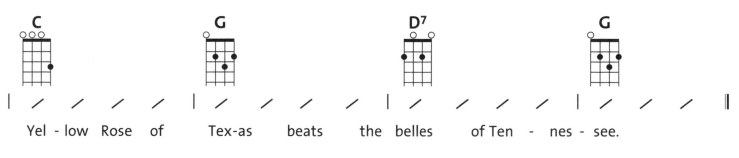

C   **G**   **D⁷**   **G**

| / / / / | / / / / | / / / / | / / / / ‖

Yel - low Rose of   Tex-as   beats   the belles   of Ten - nes - see.

1 2 3 4 5 6 7 8 9

A♭
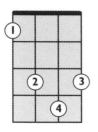

A♭⁷
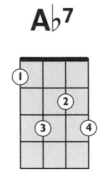

A
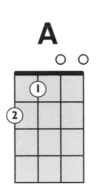

A⁷
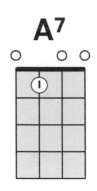

Am
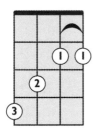

Am⁷
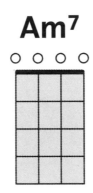

B♭
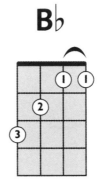

B♭⁷
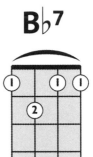

B
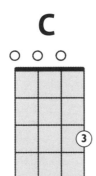

B⁷
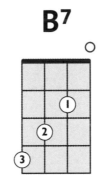

Bm
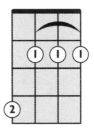

Bm⁷
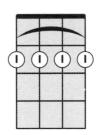

C

Cmaj⁷
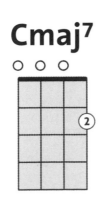

C⁷
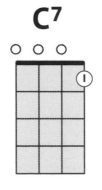

Csus⁴
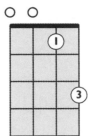

Cm

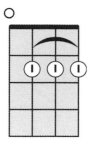

Cm⁷
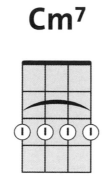

Cdim

Caug
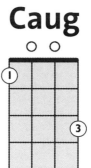

C♯

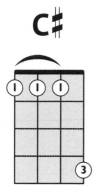

C♯⁷

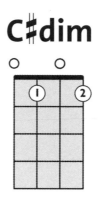

C♯dim
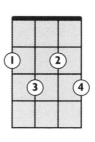

D

D⁷

Dsus⁴
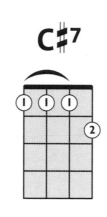

Dm

Dm⁷

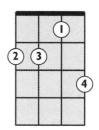

Ddim
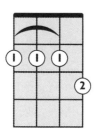

E
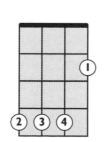

E⁷
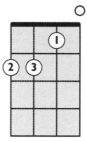

Em
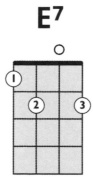

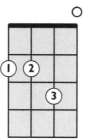
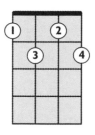
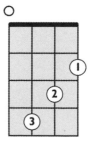
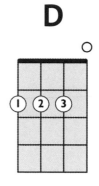

Em⁷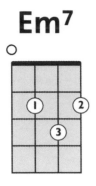

F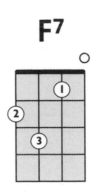

F⁷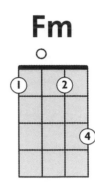

Fm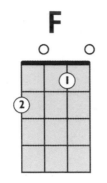

Fm⁷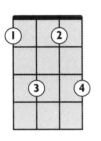

Faug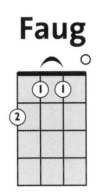

F♯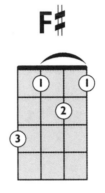

F♯7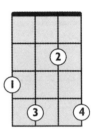

F♯m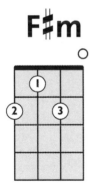

F♯m⁷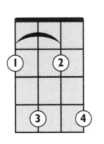

G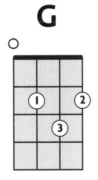

Gmaj⁷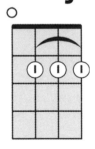

G⁷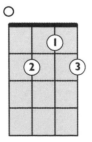

Gsus⁴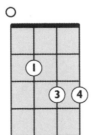

Gm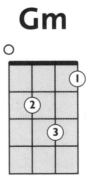

Gm⁷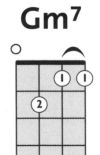